*MACMILLA*
*STORI*



# SIX TALES FROM SHAKESPEARE

## MACMILLAN STORIES TO REMEMBER SERIES
## JUNIOR TITLES

Black Beauty *by Anna Sewell*
Call of the Wild *by Jack London*
Captain Blood *by Rafael Sabatini*
Frankenstein *by Mary Shelley*
Gulliver's Travels *by Jonathan Swift*
Ivanhoe *by Sir Walter Scott*
Just-So Stories *by Rudyard Kipling*
Kim *by Rudyard Kipling*
Lorna Doone *by R.D. Blackmore*
Lost Horizon *by James Hilton*
Moby Dick *by Herman Melville*
Moonfleet *by John Meade Falkner*
National Velvet *by Enid Bagnold*
Nicholas Nickleby *by Charles Dickens*
Oliver Twist *by Charles Dickens*
Robinson Crusoe *by Daniel Defoe*
Round the World in Eighty Days *by Jules Verne*
Silas Marner *by George Eliot*
Six Short Stories
Six Tales from Shakespeare
Stories from Homer
Stange Tales from the Arabian Nights
The Adventures of Tom Sawyer *by Mark Twain*
The Mayor of Casterbridge *by Charles Dickens*
The Turn of the Screw *by Henry James*
The Vicar of Wakefield *by Oliver Goldsmith*
Tom Brown's Schooldays *by Thomas Hughes*
Treasure Island *by R.L. Stevenson*
Wonder Tales from Greece

## MODERN STORIES TO REMEMBER

All Quiet on the Western Front *by Erich Maria Remarque*
A Passage to India *by E.M. Forster*
Cakes and Ale *by Somerset Maugham*
Goodbye, Mr Chips *by James Hilton*
On the Beach *by Nevil Shute*
The Black Cloud *by Fred Hoyle*
The Great Gatsby *by F. Scott Fitzgerald*
The Gun *by C.S. Forester*
The Rocking Horse Winner, The White Stocking
and Strike-Pay *by D.H. Lawrence*

# SIX TALES FROM SHAKESPEARE

TOLD BY

**E. F. DODD, B.A.**

MACMILLAN

First published 1953
Reprinted with illustrations 1954, 1955, 1956 (twice), 1957, 1959 (three times), 1960 (twice), 1961 (twice), 1962 (twice), 1963 (twice), 1964, 1965, 1966 (twice), 1967 (twice), 1968, 1970, 1971, 1972, 1973, 1974 (twice), 1976, 1977, 1979, 1982, 1983, 1984 (three times), 1985, 1986, 1987, 1988, 1989, 1990, 1991 (four times), 1993

Published by THE MACMILLAN PRESS LTD
London and Basingstoke
*Associated companies and representatives in Accra, Auckland, Delhi, Dublin, Gaborone, Hamburg, Harare, Hong Kong, Kuala Lumpur, Lagos, Manzini, Melbourne, Mexico City, Nairobi, New York, Singapore, Tokyo.*

ISBN 0 – 333 – 07612 – 5

Printed in Hong Kong

Cover photograph by courtesy of
Holte Photographics Ltd.

# PREFACE

This book has been specially adapted for those for whom English is a second or foreign language, and who have reached at least a lower intermediate level. It will be suitable, in fact, for anyone who finds the original plays too long or too difficult.

These tales from Shakespeare are told within a vocabulary of two thousand words and the greatest care has been taken to see that no difficult sentence structures are used. At the same time, the more famous speeches have been quoted as nearly as possible to give students an early familiarity with Shakespeare's own words.

# CONTENTS

## *COMEDIES*



## *TRAGEDIES*

# THE MERCHANT OF VENICE

## PEOPLE IN THE STORY

ANTONIO, a merchant of Venice.
BASSANIO, his friend.
GRATIANO, another friend.
PORTIA, a rich lady in love with Bassanio.
NERISSA, her servant, in love with Gratiano.
SHYLOCK, a Jewish money-lender.
JESSICA, his daughter.
LORENZO, in love with Jessica.
DUKE OF VENICE.
MOROCCO } who wish to marry Portia.
ARRAGON }

Long ago, there lived in Venice, a town in Italy, a man called Antonio. He was a merchant, owning many ships which traded with distant countries; and he was a good man as well as a rich one.

Antonio's greatest friend was a young soldier, Bassanio, who loved a beautiful lady called Portia. But Bassanio was not a wealthy man, and he did not like to ask Portia to marry him, because she was as rich as she was beautiful. At last, however, he asked Antonio to lend him some money, so that he could visit Portia at Belmont, where she lived, and at least find out if she loved him.

It happened that at this time all Antonio's ships were at sea, and until they returned he had no money to lend Bassanio.

'But go to a money-lender,' he said to his friend. 'Borrow the money you need from him, and tell him that, when my ships come in, I will pay him back all that he has lent you.'

Now, there lived in Venice an old Jew named Shylock. The Jews in those days were the money-lenders of Venice. They lent money, but they forced people to pay so heavily for the loan that the Jews themselves became very rich. Shylock was one of the greediest Jews in Venice. Antonio hated him for his wicked ways, and he had often insulted the Jew and spoken rudely to him. For this reason, Shylock hated Antonio, too, and was anxious to revenge the insults.

Bassanio, knowing that Shylock was very rich, went to him to borrow the money he needed. Shylock was delighted when he heard that Antonio had promised to pay back the loan. He thought that his enemy had been given into his hands, and he made a wicked plan. He pretended to be generous, and said he would lend Bassanio the money and would not charge him anything for the loan.

'But Antonio must pay me back in three months,' Shylock said. 'And, just for a joke, he must sign a bond promising that I may cut off a pound of flesh from his body if the money is not paid.'

Bassanio had no faith in Shylock, and did not like Antonio to make such a terrible promise; but Antonio thought that Shylock was really joking, and he said: 'I am indeed content to sign such a promise. Do not be afraid, Bassanio. My ships will return a month before the money is due, and then I shall have three times as much as Shylock has lent to you.' And Antonio signed the bond.

'I do not like this promise,' said Bassanio uneasily, but Antonio said again: 'You need have no fear. My ships will come home a month before the day.'

So Bassanio unwillingly took the money, said goodbye to Antonio, and sailed away to Belmont. He took one of his friends with him, a young man called Gratiano.

The beautiful Portia lived in a big house in Belmont with her servant-companion, Nerissa. Her father had died recently and had left her a great deal of money. He had been a wise old man, and, to protect his daughter from greedy men who might try to marry her because she was so rich, he left Portia three boxes. One of the boxes contained her picture, and whoever chose this box was to be Portia's husband.

Just before Bassanio arrived from Venice, a king's son came from Africa to visit Portia. This man, Morocco, was powerful and wealthy, and he wished to marry her; but Portia did not love him and she hoped that he would choose the wrong box.

'Is it not hard, Nerissa?' she confided to her

servant. 'I cannot choose the man I wish to marry, or refuse those I dislike.'

'You have plenty of admirers to choose from,' Nerissa said. 'But do you remember a young man from Venice who once visited your father?'

'Yes, yes,' Portia answered. 'It was Bassanio—I think that was his name?'

'True, madam,' said Nerissa. 'And I think he deserved your love more than any of the others.'

'I remember him well, and I remember he was worthy of your praise,' said Portia sadly. 'But I cannot marry him unless he comes and chooses the right box.'

'Perhaps he will,' Nerissa comforted her. 'Your father was a wise and virtuous man. I am sure he will have arranged the boxes so that the right man will choose the picture.'

Nerissa's sensible suggestion made Portia feel more cheerful as she showed the three boxes to the dark-skinned African from Morocco. He examined them carefully, and read the words written on the outside of each one. On the gold box was written:

*Whoever chooses me shall gain what*
*many men desire.*

On the silver box was written:

*Whoever chooses me shall get as much*
*as he deserves.*

And on the plain box, made of lead, was written:

*Whoever chooses me must give and risk*
*all that he has.*

'What many men desire,' Morocco said, looking at the golden box. 'That must be the fair Portia, and her picture will certainly be inside a box of gold.'

He opened it, but all he found inside was an ugly skull[1], and a piece of paper containing these words:

*All that shines is not gold. Goodbye!*

So Morocco sadly said goodbye to Portia and returned to Africa.

The next visitor was the prince of Arragon, and he, too, was shown the three boxes. Arragon was a vain young man with a very high opinion of himself, and he chose the silver box.

'If I get as much as I deservc,' he said, 'I shall certainly gain the fair Portia.'

But the box contained nothing but a fool's head and these words:

*Many fools are hidden behind a silver covering.*
*So be gone, sir!*

The prince, feeling very silly, went away as sadly as Morocco had done.

Then Bassanio and Gratiano arrived, and Bassanio begged Portia to permit him to try his luck with the three boxes. She was very much afraid that he might choose the wrong box, but she dared not tell

[1]*skull: the bones of a head.*

He looked at the box of gold and the box of silver, and shook his head

him which was the right one. He looked at the box of gold and the box of silver, and shook his head.

'The things which are most beautiful outside are often the ugliest within,' he said. 'I choose the plain lead box.'

Portia was filled with joy as Bassanio opened the box and found inside a lovely picture of her. They arranged to be married at once, and Bassanio's friend, Gratiano, asked for permission to marry Nerissa at the same time.

But their happiness was soon disturbed by bad news. A ship arrived from Venice, bringing a friend of Bassanio's called Lorenzo. With Lorenzo was his wife, Jessica, the beautiful daughter of Shylock the Jew. Shylock had always been harsh and cruel to Jessica, and she knew he would never consent to her marrying Lorenzo; first, because he was not a Jew, and secondly because he was a friend of Antonio's. So one night she ran away from her father's house to marry Lorenzo, taking with her a great deal of money and some jewels.

They had come to Belmont to escape Shylock's anger, and they brought with them a letter to Bassanio from Antonio. Bassanio read the letter, and he turned so pale that Portia feared that his friend must be dead.

'What is it, Bassanio?' she asked anxiously. 'You must let me share the bad news that this letter brings.'

'Oh, sweet Portia,' said Bassanio. 'Here are some of the most unpleasant words that have ever been written.'

The letter told him that Antonio's six ships, full of riches, had all been wrecked at sea, and Antonio's money had been lost with them. And this was not all. Shylock hated Antonio more than ever since his friend, Lorenzo, had run away with Jessica. He was so angry at the loss of his daughter and his money that he walked the streets crying: 'My daughter! My money! My jewels! Justice, justice! Find me my money and my daughter!' And when he heard that all Antonio's ships were lost, he was very glad. Now he could revenge himself on

Antonio and on all those who loved the brave young merchant.

Shylock went to the Duke of Venice and told him of Antonio's bargain and of the letter he had signed. The Duke and many of the merchants tried to persuade Shylock to give up his cruel revenge, but he would not listen to them.

'Antonio cannot pay the money,' said Shylock. 'He must therefore keep his promise and pay me the pound of flesh.'

Jessica had heard her father tell his Jewish friends that he would rather have a pound of Antonio's flesh than be paid twenty times the sum that was owed to him.

Bassanio was terribly disturbed by the news, and decided that he must return at once to Venice to try to save his friend. Portia had a kind and generous heart, and did not try to prevent his going.

'Let us be married now,' she said. 'And then you must go to Venice at once. You shall have gold to pay this debt twenty times over: and when it is paid, bring your true friend here.'

So they were married, and after the ceremony Bassanio and Gratiano set off at once for Venice. They found that the trial was just beginning.

Antonio did not ask for mercy. He knew that Shylock hated him too much to be merciful. Besides, a man must keep his promise; otherwise people would think that the merchants of Venice were not honest men.

The Duke of Venice, who was judging the case, begged Shylock to be merciful.

'Why should I be merciful?' said the Jew. 'I do not love Antonio.'

'Do all men kill the things they do not love? asked Bassanio angrily.

'Don't all men want to kill the thing they hate?' answered Shylock bitterly.

'I will give you twice as much as Antonio owes you, if you will let him go free,' Bassanio said.

'If you offered me six thousand times more than the amount he owes me, I should still ask for my pound of flesh,' the Jew replied.

'How can you hope for mercy if you show none?' asked the Duke, but Shylock answered violently:

'I do not want mercy. I want justice. Give me my pound of flesh.' He bcgan to sharpen the long knife he had brought with him, feeling that his revenge was very near.

But at that moment a messenger came to the Duke with the news that a clever young lawyer had arrived from another town to judge the case. Almost at once the lawyer entered, accompanied by his clerk. They both looked very young, but they brought with them a written introduction from a lawyer friend of the Duke's who assured him that the young man was well qualified to judge the case.

His wisdom was soon shown by the careful questions he asked the Jew. When he had heard all that Shylock and Antonio had to say, he begged the Jew to be merciful.

'Why should I be merciful? Tell me that!' shouted Shylock angrily; and the young lawyer made a fine speech, telling Shylock of the value of mercy.

'Mercy is twice-blessed,' he said. 'It blesses him who gives and him who receives. Great kings are always merciful; and God himself is known to be full of gentleness and mercy. Therefore, Jew, although you ask for justice, I ask you to be merciful.'

Shylock would not listen. He could think of nothing but revenge, and he refused to take the money Bassanio offered, although Bassanio said he would give him ten times the sum he owed.

'Come, Shylock,' said the lawyer patiently. 'Be merciful. Take three times the sum and let me tear up the promise.'

Shylock still refused, and the lawyer had to admit that his claim was right according to the law of Venice; and, if the Jew would not be merciful, Antonio must give him his pound of flesh.

'A wise man come to judgment! Oh, wise young judge, how I admire you!' cried Shylock, bringing out his knife again.

'You must prepare yourself for the knife,' the lawyer said to Antonio.

'Oh, noble judge! Oh, wonderful young man!' cried Shylock.

'Come, open up your coat,' said the lawyer.

'Yes, yes—his coat, nearest the heart, noble judge!' said Shylock, feeling the sharp edge of his knife.

'Are there balances here to weigh the flesh?' asked the young man.

'I have them ready,' answered Shylock.

'Have you called a doctor, to stop his wounds in case he bleeds to death?'

'No,' said Shylock. 'That is not written in the bond.'

The young judge asked Antonio if he had anything to say. Antonio told Bassanio that he loved him greatly and was glad to die for his sake and then he said goodbye.

'No,' said Shylock. 'That is not written in the bond'

'A pound of this merchant's flesh is yours,' said the lawyer to Shylock. 'The court agrees, and the law admits it.'

'Most rightful judge!' said the delighted Jew.

'And you must cut this flesh from near his heart; the law admits it, and the court agrees.'

'Most learned judge!' said Shylock. 'Come, Antonio, prepare yourself.'

'Wait a little,' said the judge. 'There is something else. This letter does not promise you one drop of blood. Take your pound of flesh; but if you spill one drop of blood you must give all your money and possessions to the State.'

Now it was Gratiano's turn to praise the lawyer.

'Oh, learned judge!' he cried. 'Listen, Shylock, to the learned judge!'

'You asked for justice, and you shall have it,' said the lawyer.

'Then,' cried Shylock hastily, 'give me the money, Bassanio. Give me three times what Antonio owes me, as you said you would.'

'Not so fast!' said the judge. 'You have already refused the money. You shall have justice, but nothing else.'

Finally, shaking with anger, the old Jew asked for the money he had lent Bassanio, and no more. But the judge refused him.

'And we have not finished yet,' he continued. 'You, Shylock, are a Jew. According to the laws of Venice, if anyone who is not himself a citizen of

Venice tries to take the life of a true citizen, he must be put to death; and his money and property must be shared equally between the State and the man he has tried to kill. You are not a citizen of Venice, and you have tried to kill Antonio. The Duke must decide on your punishment.'

'I shall show you more mercy than you showed Antonio,' said the Duke to the frightened Jew. 'I give you your life, but your money must be given to Antonio and the State.'

Shylock was a defeated man. What could he, a money-lender, do if all his money was taken from him?

'Take my life as well!' he cried bitterly. 'You take my life, anyway, if you take the means by which I live.'

The young judge turned to Antonio and said:

'What mercy can you offer him, Antonio?'

And kind-hearted Antonio, pitying the broken old man, said gently: 'Let him keep my share of the property, but on one condition. When he dies, he must leave all his possessions to his daughter Jessica and her husband.'

'Are you contented, Shylock? What do you say?' asked the lawyer.

'I am content,' said Shylock. 'And now, I pray you, give me leave to go. I am not well. Send me the papers and I will sign them.' And the old Jew left the court.

Antonio and Bassanio were full of gratitude to

the clever young judge, and asked him to accept the money that Shylock had lent Bassanio. But the judge would not take it, saying he was well paid by their content.

'Then, dear sir,' said Bassanio, 'take some small gift to remind you of our gratitude.'

'If you insist,' said the young man, 'I will take the ring you wear on your finger.'

Bassanio hastily drew back his hand, because the ring was one that Portia had given him, and he had promised her that he would keep it always. He told the judge the ring was of small value, and promised he would buy him a more expensive one instead.

But the young man seemed annoyed.

'You taught me how to beg,' he said. 'And now, I think you teach me how a beggar should be answered.' He said goodbye coldly to Bassanio and went away.

When he had gone, however, Antonio persuaded Bassanio to let the lawyer have the ring, and Bassanio—regretting his earlier refusal—sent Gratiano to find the young judge and give it to him. Poor Gratiano found himself in trouble, too: because, after giving Bassanio's ring to the lawyer, he was persuaded by the lawyer's clerk to give him his own ring—a gift to him from Nerissa at their marriage.

Bassanio and Gratiano returned to Belmont, taking Antonio with them. They were full of happiness at the thought of seeing Portia and Nerissa again, but they were a little worried. What would their wives say to them when they noticed that the rings had gone?

When Portia looked at Bassanio's hand, she asked him at once what had happened to his ring. He explained, but she seemed very annoyed. He begged her to forgive him, and Antonio told her that Bassanio was not to blame. He had given the ring to the clever lawyer who had saved Antonio's life.

'I dare swear he will never again break a promise to you,' Antonio said.

'Then give him this ring,' said Portia, 'and tell him to keep it better than the other.'

To Bassanio's astonishment, she gave him the very same ring that he had given to the judge. And Nerissa returned to Gratiano the ring which he had given to the lawyer's clerk.

'You are all amazed!' said Portia, laughing at their puzzled faces. 'But here is a letter. Read it, all of you. There you will find that Portia was the lawyer, and Nerissa was her clerk.'

'Were you the lawyer, and I did not know you?' Bassanio asked in amazement.

'Yes,' Portia said. 'Lorenzo will tell you that I have only just returned from Venice.' She turned to Antonio. 'Antonio, you are welcome,' she said. 'And I have better news for you than you expect. Three of your ships have arrived safely back in harbour, and your money is safe.'

And so there were great rejoicings at the house at

Belmont, and all was well for Antonio, the brave young merchant of Venice.

## QUESTIONS

1. Why did Bassanio want to borrow money from his friend, Antonio? Why could Antonio not lend him the money?
2. What payment did Shylock demand if Antonio could not pay back the money?
3. What were Portia's three boxes made of, and who chose the one containing her picture?
4. Why did Shylock not dare to cut the pound of flesh from Antonio's heart?
5. What gift did Bassanio give to the young judge?

## THE TAMING OF THE SHREW

### PEOPLE IN THE STORY

BAPTISTA, a rich gentleman of Padua.
KATHARINE, the Shrew } daughters of Baptista.
BIANCA }
HORTENSIO } in love with Bianca.
LUCENTIO }
PETRUCHIO
VINCENTIO, father of Lucentio.

In Padua, a beautiful city of Italy, there once lived a rich gentleman called Baptista. He had two daughters, the gentle and beautiful Bianca, and Katharine. Katharine was as beautiful as her sister, but she had such an ungovernable temper that she was always known as Katharine the Shrew. Everyone was afraid of her angry tongue, and in spite of her beautiful face she had no admirers.

Katharine was Baptista's elder daughter, and he began to fear that she would never find a husband. Many men wanted to marry Bianca, but no one was willing to risk marriage with the bad-tempered Katharine. At last Baptista decided on a plan. He announced that Katharine must be married before Bianca; it was the elder sister's right. Bianca's admirers at once began to look round for a man who would be brave enough to marry this wild cat, ' Katharine the cursed.'

Now, in Verona, another Italian town, there lived a rich and gay young man called Petruchio. His father had recently died and left him plenty of money, and Petruchio now wished to see the world and find a wife. So he went to Padua, and there he met a friend, Hortensio, one of the young men who wanted to marry Bianca. Petruchio told him that he, too, was looking for a wife, and Hortensio at once thought of Katharine the Shrew. Petruchio was a strong-willed young man; surely he would be able to make Katharine obey him? He was merry and good-tempered, too, and clever and amusing. Altogether, he was a wise young man, and would know how to tame an ill-tempered wife.

So Hortensio told Petruchio all about the gentle Bianca, whom he loved and wished to marry; and about the beautiful but bad-tempered Katharine.

' And no one can marry Bianca until Katharine has a husband,' he finished sadly.

Petruchio was interested and amused.

' I'll marry her,' he said. ' Let her scold as loudly as a thunderstorm! I shall still make her love me.'

And he went to Baptista's house, taking Hortensio with him.

' You must pretend to be a musician,' Petruchio said to him. ' You can teach Katharine music and

I will teach her love. Between us we will tame the shrew.'

When they reached Baptista's house Petruchio spoke to him at once.

'Pray, have you not a daughter called Katharine, fair and virtuous?' he asked.

'I have a daughter, sir, called Katharine,' Baptista answered.

'I am a gentleman of Verona, sir,' Petruchio went on. 'I have heard so much of the beauty and gentleness of your daughter Katharine that I have come to ask your permission for my friend to teach her music and for me to marry her.'

'You are very welcome' Baptista said, and he sent Hortensio to Katharine at once. 'But I am afraid my daughter would not suit you,' he added sadly to Petruchio.

'I see you do not wish to part with her, or else you do not want me for a son-in-law,' said Petruchio.

'Indeed, you are mistaken,' said Baptista. 'But where do you live, sir? What is your name?'

When Baptista heard his name, he realised that Petruchio's father was an old friend of his, and he welcomed the young man gladly to his house. But he had to admit that he doubted whether his elder daughter would make Petruchio a good wife; even her father was afraid of her scolding tongue. 'I wish you good luck with her,' he said to the young man, 'but you must be prepared for some unhappy words.'

At this moment, Hortensio came running into the room. His head was cut and bleeding, and his face was white with fear and anger.

'Why are you so pale?' asked Baptista. 'What is the matter? Will my daughter prove a good musician?'

'She will make a better soldier,' said Hortensio angrily. He told Baptista that he had tried to correct Katharine's playing on the lute[1], and she had grown so angry that she had struck him on the head with the instrument. His head was cut and the lute was broken; and while he stood helplessly in front of her she had shouted at him rudely, calling him by insulting names.

Petruchio thought this was a huge joke, and burst out laughing.

'She is a brave girl!' he said, delighted. 'I love her ten times more than ever.' He told Baptista how impatient he was to meet this merry Katharine, and asked if he could see her at once. So Baptista advised the unhappy Hortensio to go and find Bianca, who would prove an easier pupil; and Baptista himself went to fetch the stormy Katharine. Petruchio, left alone, decided on his treatment of this wild and angry girl.

'If she scolds, I shall tell her that she sings as sweetly as a bird,' thought he. 'If she frowns, I'll say she looks as clear as morning roses newly washed with dew. If she will not speak a word, I shall say

---

[1] *lute: a small stringed musical instrument.*

how well she talks. If she tells me to be gone, I shall thank her as if she had asked me to stay a week. If she will not marry me, I shall ask her to name the day for our marriage.'

The proud Katharine entered, annoyed with this stranger who had asked to see her, but Petruchio made no apology. He greeted her cheerfully with the words:

'Good-morrow, Kate, for that's your name, I hear.'

'They call me Katharine that do talk of me,' said Katharine angrily.

'You lie!' said Petruchio. 'You are called plain Kate, and pretty Kate, and sometimes Kate the cursed; but, Kate, you are the prettiest Kate in all the world. Your beauty, your gentleness, and your virtues are praised in every town, and I have come to ask you to be my wife.'

'How dare you!' Katharine cried. 'Will you go away at once!'

But Petruchio would not go. Katharine argued with him, she scolded him, she tried to make him quarrel; but he pretended not to hear her insults. He praised her beauty and her gentle ways and said that those who had told him she was a bad-tempered shrew were liars. Finally he said: 'Sweet Kate, I am going to marry you whether you wish it or not. Your father has given his consent, and I shall tame you, Kate, and change you from a wild Kate to a gentle Kate. Here comes your father: never make denial. I must and will have Katharine for my wife.'

And when Baptista came in, Petruchio told him that he and Katharine had arranged to be married on the following Sunday.

'I'll see you hanged on Sunday before I marry you,' cried Katharine, stamping her foot in anger, and she accused her father of wishing to marry her to a madman. But Petruchio interrupted her stormy speech.

'Be patient,' he said to Baptista. 'She talks like this when you are here, but when we are alone she is most gentle and loving. Indeed, you will not believe how much she loves me.' Then turning to Katharine, he said: 'Come, kiss me, Kate! I will go to Venice to buy fine clothes and jewels, for we will be married on Sunday.'

And Katharine, speechless with anger and astonishment at this extraordinary young man's behaviour, said no more.

On Sunday the feast was ready and the guests arrived. Katharine was frowning and bad-tempered, but she was dressed in fine new clothes and was ready for the marriage. Everyone was waiting for Petruchio, but he did not come. The guests whispered to each other, and Katharine cursed and scolded, and then ran tearfully out of the room—ashamed because Petruchio had treated her so badly.

'He never means to marry me,' she cried. 'He has done all this to make a fool of me.'

By this time everyone was certain that Petruchio would not come, but suddenly he rode up on an ancient horse which was so thin and ill that it could hardly walk. Petruchio himself looked like a beggar, in torn and dirty clothes, with a rusty, broken sword at his belt; and his servant was dressed in the same untidy fashion. The guests whispered together in astonishment as Petruchio jumped down from his miserable horse, calling: 'Where is Kate? Where is my lovely wife?'

Baptista was extremely annoyed with Petruchio for keeping them all waiting, and for arriving in such a disgraceful state. 'Why, sir, you know this is your wedding day,' he said, and told Petruchio to go and change into more suitable clothes at once.

Petruchio, however, stubbornly refused to change anything. 'Kate is marrying me, not my clothes,' he said.

All arguments proved useless, and at last Katharine went unwillingly to church. During the ceremony, Petruchio continued to act in the same wild and shocking way. He cursed the priest so loudly that the poor man dropped his book in astonishment, and, when he bent down to pick it up, Petruchio rudely knocked him over. He continued to curse and shout and stamp his feet, and poor Katharine, who had never been afraid of anyone, began to tremble with fear. When the ceremony was over, Petruchio called loudly for a cup of wine, drank half of it, and threw the remains into the priest's face.

'His beard looked so thin and hungry,' Petruchio said, roaring with laughter. 'I thought some wine would do it good.'

At last Katharine succeeded in persuading him to return to her father's house, but Petruchio told her that it was impossible for them to remain for the marriage feast.

'Please stay for the feast!' Katharine begged him. 'What will our guests say if we go away now?'

But Petruchio did not care about the guests, and refused to stay.

'If you love me, stay,' Katharine said again.

Petruchio's only answer was to tell his servant to bring the horses, and Katharine flew into a temper.

'Go, then!' she cried. 'The door is open. But I will not go today; no, nor tomorrow, nor till I wish to go.'

'Oh, Kate, do not be angry,' said Petruchio.

'I will be angry!' said angry Katharine. 'You shall stay as long as I wish.' And she turned to the guests. 'Gentlemen,' she said. 'Let us go forward to the dinner. I see a woman may be made a fool, if she does not have the spirit to resist.'

'*They* shall go forward, Kate, at your command,' said Petruchio. 'Go, gentlemen, feast as my wife tells you. But my pretty Kate must go with me. I will be master of my own wife.'

And Kate could do no more. Before she realized what was happening, she found herself riding with Petruchio to his home. It was a tiring ride, because Petruchio had chosen the worst roads for their journey, and their horses were old and thin. While they were coming down a steep hill, Katharine's horse fell down in the mud, with Katharine underneath it. Petruchio, instead of helping his wife to get up, began to beat his servant, blaming him for the horse's fall. Katharine struggled up and tried to pull her husband away from the servant, and such a noise and confusion followed! Petruchio shouted, and Katharine argued, and the servant cried for mercy; and when they at last grew calmer they found that the horses had run away. At last the servant caught the horses, and Katharine—tired and hungry, with mud-stained clothes—reached her new home. She was quite sure, by this time, that she had married a madman; and her troubles were not yet ended. When the servants came out of the house to welcome them, Petruchio cursed and scolded them all, and Katharine begged him to be more gentle with them.

Supper was brought, and Petruchio criticised every dish. He grumbled that the food was burned and badly cooked, and quite unfit to eat. Katharine could find nothing wrong with it and she was extremely hungry, but Petruchio would not let her eat. No, the meat was bad, he said. It would make her ill. And he threw the food on the floor.

Katharine was tired out and nearly in tears, but even when she went to bed she was not allowed to rest. Petruchio continued to find fault with everything in the bedroom. He said the bed was not fit for her to sleep in, and he threw the bedclothes on the floor. All night long he shouted and complained so loudly that Katharine could not sleep. She did not realize that this was part of Petruchio's plan to cure her of her angry tempers. He intended to show her how miserable it was to live with someone who was continually scolding and grumbling. When she realized this, she would soon mend her bad-tempered ways; but, meanwhile, she was very unhappy.

Next day, Petruchio behaved in the same way—always speaking gently to his wife, but making everything as uncomfortable for her as he could. By this time she was so hungry that she begged a servant to bring her some food; but he made excuses and at last he told her that he dare not bring her food without his master's orders.

'Did he marry me to starve me?' Katharine asked angrily. 'Beggars who come to my father's door are given food. But I, who do not know how to beg, am starved for meat, and tired from lack of sleep. I was kept awake all night by Petruchio's shouting. And it annoys me most of all that he pretends to do all this because he loves me.'

Just then Petruchio came in, carrying a dish of meat.

‘How are you, my sweet Kate?’ he asked. ‘See how much I think about your comfort. I myself have cooked some food for you.’

Katharine did not answer.

‘No thanks?’ said Petruchio. ‘What, not a word? Perhaps you do not like the food?’ And he ordered the servant to take the meat away.

‘No! No! Let it stay!’ cried Katharine, who was weak with hunger.

‘The poorest service is repaid with thanks; and you must thank me before you touch the meat,’ said Petruchio.

‘I thank you, sir,’ said Katharine miserably, and Petruchio allowed her to have a little of the meat. But before she had finished he pretended to think that she had had enough, and told the servant to take the dish away.

He then sent for a tailor to bring some clothes which he had ordered for her. The tailor showed Katharine a beautiful cap.

‘What a cap!’ said Petruchio. ‘It is much too small. It is like a baby's cap! Come, let us have a bigger one.’

‘I do not want a bigger one!’ cried poor Katharine. ‘This one is the fashion, and gentlewomen wear such caps as these.’

‘When you are gentle, you shall have one, too,’ replied her annoying husband.

Katharine lost her temper.

‘I hope I may have permission to speak, and

speak I will!' she cried. 'I am no child, no baby, to be treated like this. Other people have listened to me, and if you cannot, you had better stop your ears.'

'It is quite true what you say,' said Petruchio, taking absolutely no notice of her words. 'It is a silly cap. I love you because you do not like it.'

'Love me or love me not,' said Katharine. 'I like that cap and I will have it!'

'Take it away, tailor, we do not want it,' said Petruchio. 'Now, let us see the dress.' He picked up the dress and examined it. 'Oh, what cheap material!' he went on. 'What in the world, tailor, do you call this? You have cut the cloth so badly that the dress is spoiled.'

'I have never seen a nicer dress,' said Katharine. 'I admire it in every way.'

But Petruchio would not listen to her, and told the tailor to take the clothes away. Privately he told the servants to keep the dress and cap for Katharine, and to pay the tailor's bill; but he said to Katharine: 'Well, come, my Kate. We shall have to go to your father's house in the poor clothes we are wearing now.'

He ordered the servants to bring the horses, saying that it was now seven o'clock and they would easily reach Baptista's house in time for dinner. But the time was really two o'clock in the afternoon, and Katharine told him so.

'It will be supper-time before we arrive there,' she said gently.

‘You argue with everything I say!’ said Petruchio crossly. ‘All right. I shall not go today. But when I go, the time will be whatever I say it is.’

Next day, Katharine had learned her lesson and she did not argue with Petruchio about the time of day. They set out on horseback to her father’s house. After some time they decided to get down from their horses and rest. It was a lovely morning: the sun was shining, and there was not a cloud in the sky.

‘How brightly the moon is shining,’ said Petruchio.

‘The moon?’ said Katharine. ‘The sun, you mean! It is not moonlight now.’

‘I say it is the moon that shines so brightly,’ Petruchio repeated.

‘I know it is the sun,’ Katharine insisted unwisely.

‘Now, by my mother’s son (and that’s myself),’ said Petruchio, ‘it shall be moon, or star, or what I please, before I travel to your father’s house.’

‘I shall never be able to please this man!’ thought Katharine sadly.

‘Let us go forward!’ she said to Petruchio. ‘It shall be the moon, or the sun, or whatever you please. I will not argue with you.’

‘I say, then, it is the moon,’ said Petruchio again.

‘I know it is the moon,’ answered Katharine.

‘No, then, you lie. It is the blessed sun,’ said her husband.

Presently an old gentleman came along the road

'All right, it is the blessed sun,' said Katharine in despair. 'I will agree with everything you say.'

Presently an old gentleman came along the road, and—to test Katharine's new obedience—Petruchio said to the old man:

'Good morning, gentle lady.' Then, turning to Katharine, he remarked: 'Tell me truly, sweet Kate, did you ever see a fairer lady?'

He praised the old gentleman's soft, fair skin, and said his eyes were like stars.

'Sweet Kate, kiss this lovely maid, for her beauty's sake,' he said.

Katharine had really learned her lesson this time.

'Fair, fresh, and sweet young maid,' she said

solemnly to the old man, 'Where are you going? Where is your home? How happy your parents must be, to have so fair a child.'

The old man looked at her in great astonishment, and Petruchio said sharply: 'Why, now, Kate—I hope you are not mad. This is an old man, and not a young girl, as you say he is.'

'Forgive me, old father,' said Kate. 'The sun was shining in my eyes and I could not see you properly. Please excuse my mad mistake.'

The old gentleman, whose name was Vincentio, replied that he was going to Padua, and he joined them on their journey. He told them he was visiting his son, Lucentio, who was going to marry Katharine's lovely sister, Bianca. (Petruchio's friend, the musician Hortensio, had been unsuccessful with Bianca, but had already married another woman.)

Katharine and Petruchio and the old man arrived just in time for Bianca's marriage feast, and Petruchio was delighted to find that Hortensio was also there with his newly-married wife. When the meal was finished and the ladies had left the room, the men began to joke with Petruchio about his bad-tempered wife. Even Baptista said to him sadly: 'Indeed I think, son Petruchio, that you have married the worst shrew of them all.'

'And I say no!' said Petruchio boldly. 'And we will prove it. Let each man send for his wife, and we will see whose wife is most obedient.'

Lucentio and Hortensio gladly agreed to do this, both being confident of their gentle wives' obedience. Lucentio first sent a servant to ask Bianca to come.

In a few minutes, however, the servant returned alone.

'My mistress sends you word that she is busy and cannot come,' he said.

'She is busy and she cannot come! Is that an answer?' laughed Petruchio. But they told him to wait his turn; his wife would send him a worse answer.

Next, Hortensio said to his servant:

'Go and beg my wife to come to me.'

'Oh ho! Beg her!' said Petruchio. 'Of course she will come if you beg her to do so.'

'I am afraid, sir,' said Hortensio, 'that your wife will not come, even if you beg her.'

But Hortensio's servant also returned alone.

'Where is my wife?' asked Hortensio in surprise.

'She says you must be joking,' answered the servant. 'She will not come. She says you must go to her.'

'Worse and worse; she will not come!' said Petruchio. 'Oh, this is not to be endured!' He turned to his servant and said: 'Go to my wife and tell her that I command her to come to me.'

'I know what her answer will be,' said Hortensio.

'What will it be?' Petruchio asked him.

'She will not come,' he answered. But he had

hardly spoken when Katharine's father cried out in surprise.

'Here comes Katharine,' he said, looking at his daughter in astonishment, because Katharine's manner was neither angry nor ill-tempered. She went quietly to her husband and asked him gently: 'What is your will, sir? Did you send for me?'

'Where is your sister, and Hortensio's wife?' asked Petruchio.

'They are sitting talking by the fire,' Katharine answered.

'Go bring them here,' Petruchio told her, and Katharine went at once to call them.

'Here is a wonder!' cried Lucentio.

'And so it is,' Hortensio agreed. 'I wonder what it means?'

'It means peace,' said Petruchio, smiling. 'And love, and a quiet life. In short, it means all that is sweet and happy. And if you will wait a little, I will show you more signs of her obedience.'

Katharine soon returned with the other two wives, and Petruchio said to her: 'Katharine, that cap of yours does not suit you. Take it off and throw it away.'

At once Katharine took off her cap and threw it on the ground.

Bianca and Hortensio's wife looked at her in amazement.

'How silly you are!' they cried. 'We should never obey our husbands in such stupid commands.'

'Katharine,' said Petruchio. 'Tell these foolish women how they should behave towards their husbands.'

And, to everyone's amazement, Katharine talked wisely and gently to the other wives about the duties of a wife. When she had finished, Petruchio kissed her proudly.

'Why, there's a girl!' he said.

'He has tamed a shrew!' whispered the others.

And Katharine was no longer called the Shrew. She continued to be a loving, kind and dutiful wife, and Petruchio lived proudly and happily with his own sweet Kate.

## QUESTIONS

1. A shrew is a scolding, bad-tempered woman. Who was called the Shrew?
2. Why did Bianca's admirers try so hard to find a husband for Katharine?
3. At their first meeting, how did Petruchio treat all Katharine's rudeness? Did he quarrel with her?
4. After they were married, why did Petruchio behave so badly?
5. Did he tame the Shrew?

# THE TEMPEST

## PEOPLE IN THE STORY

PROSPERO, the real Duke of Milan.
ANTONIO, his brother, who has made himself the Duke.
MIRANDA, Prospero's daughter.
ALONSO, King of Naples.
SEBASTIAN, his brother.
FERDINAND, Alonso's son.
GONZALO, an honest old nobleman.
ARIEL, a fairy.
CALIBAN, a slave.

ONCE, long ago, in the far-away country of Italy, there was a Duke of Milan called Prospero. He was a wise and learned man, more interested in books than in ruling his country. He left the care of political affairs to his brother Antonio, while he himself studied strange sciences and books of magic.

Antonio, however, was jealous of his brother. He felt that while Prospero remained in Italy he would always be considered the real Duke of Milan; and Antonio wanted that title for himself. And so he and Alonso, the King of Naples, made a wicked plan; they decided to send Prospero far away from his country, so that Antonio could rule Milan in his place.

One dark, stormy night Prospero was secretly

taken prisoner by his enemies and carried down to the sea-shore. His little three-year-old daughter, Miranda, was taken with him, and they were put into an old boat which had neither sails nor oars. Antonio had ordered that they were to take nothing with them—not even food; he was certain that the old boat would sink in the stormy seas, and Prospero and Miranda would be drowned. He did not dare to murder them in Milan, knowing how greatly they were loved by all the people.

There was, however, one kind old man among Alonso's noblemen, whose name was Gonzalo. He secretly put food and warm clothes and water into the boat; and he added some of Prospero's books, knowing the Duke's love for his library.

The little boat was pushed out to sea, and for many hours it rocked helplessly on the waves. The small Miranda was too young to be afraid, and she slept peacefully in the bottom of the boat; but Prospero began to doubt whether they would ever see land again. At last the storm ended and the sea was calm once more. Perhaps Prospero's magic had something to do with it, for he was a very clever man, practised in the arts of magic. Perhaps the good fairies were watching over him and his little daughter. Whatever the cause, when morning came Prospero saw an island in the sea ahead of him, and soon he managed to steer the boat to the sandy shore. He landed safely and carried the sleeping Miranda to a sheltered cave;

then he returned to the boat to fetch their clothes and his precious books. Those books were a great help to him in the years that followed.

There seemed to be no one living on the island, but it was rich and green, with a plentiful supply of fruit and vegetables, and fresh streams of water. Prospero decided that he and his little daughter would be able to live there in happiness and comfort for as long as was necessary. He soon discovered, too, that there were fairies on the island, and he was glad that he had spent so many years in studying magic. His knowledge gave him power over all these strange creatures, the chief of whom was a fairy called Ariel. Prospero found Ariel quite by chance, when he was walking through the woods one day. He heard a voice crying pitifully from inside a tree, and with his magic Prospero was able to split the tree open. To his astonishment a pretty little fairy flew out from the centre of the tree.

The fairy, who said his name was Ariel, had a sad story to tell. He had been imprisoned in the tree for twelve years, through the magic of a wicked old woman called Sycorax. When Sycorax first came to the island, Ariel and many other fairies had refused to obey her, and to punish them she had imprisoned them all inside these trees. Now she was dead, and no one lived on the island except her ugly, half-mad son, Caliban.

Prospero freed all the fairies from their woody prisons, and they gratefully promised to help him faithfully in anything he ordered them to do. Prospero then went in search of the ugly Caliban. He found him hiding fearfully in a cave, and at first he tried to teach this miserable creature some of his own knowledge. He taught him the names of the sun and the moon, and fed him on berries and water and was gentle and kind to him. But Caliban was wicked, stupid and ungrateful, and finally Prospero made him his slave; he had to carry water and cut firewood, and lived in a little cave by himself.

And so Prospero and Miranda lived on this magic island, helped by the fairies and served by the ugly

Prospero and Miranda visit Caliban's cave

Caliban, who was more like a wild beast than a man.

Twelve years passed, and Miranda grew to be a beautiful girl. In all those twelve years she had never seen a human being except her father. She remembered nothing of their life in Milan, because she had been so young when they left Italy. Nor did she know that her father had once been the Duke of Milan. She was perfectly content to live on the island and asked for nothing different.

And then, one day, there was a terrible storm. Miranda stood on the shore, watching the wild waves and the heavy rain sweeping across the sea, and suddenly she saw a ship being carried by the strong tide towards the rocks. In those days there were no steam ships, and the sails of the ship were torn by the wind and great waves washed over the decks. Even above the noise of the storm Miranda could hear the sailors crying for help.

'All lost! To prayers, to prayers! Mercy on us!' she heard them cry, and she ran to tell her father. Surely he, with the fairies to help him, and with his great knowledge of magic, could do something to save the ship?

But Prospero did not seem greatly anxious about the fate of the sailors. He told Miranda that all would be well and that no harm would come to the ship. He himself had caused the storm: he intended to frighten the people on board, but they would none of them be drowned, and the ship, too, would be saved.

'But why are you doing this?' Miranda asked. 'These men have done you no harm.'

Prospero smiled at her sadly.

'Many years ago they did me great harm, my child,' he said gently. 'The time has come for me to tell you all about it. Let us sit down on this rock while you listen to my story.'

So Miranda sat at her father's feet and he told her about their life in Milan, and the reason why they were now living on this lonely island.

'I am still the rightful Duke of Milan,' he finished, 'and now my opportunity has come to revenge myself on my enemies. They are all on board that ship rolling in the waves. Alonso, the King of Naples, arranged for his daughter to marry a foreign king, and he hired this ship to carry them across the sea to Africa. The wedding is over, and they are now returning to Naples. The King's son, Ferdinand, is with his father on board; and my brother Antonio and the King's brother, Sebastian, are also with them.'

Prospero had learned all this through his strange magic powers, and he had planned the storm. With Ariel's help he arranged that the ship should be driven towards the island by the winds, and that it should seem to be wrecked on the rocky shore.

'Nobody will be hurt,' he promised his daughter. ‘But they must be punished and made to regret their unkindness to us both.’

Miranda trusted her father and knew that he would not break his promise to her, so, tired with all the excitement of the storm, she lay down and went to sleep. Then Prospero called Ariel to him, for he had more work for him to do.

Ariel had had a very busy morning and he felt tired and cross. He began to complain to his master.

‘What? Is there more work?’ he said. ‘Don’t you remember that you promised me my liberty if I served you faithfully in this matter? I have brought the ship to the island and now I want to be free.’

‘The time has not yet come,’ Prospero answered. ‘Have you forgotten how I saved you from a terrible imprisonment? Do you want to be locked in that tree again? If you will serve me for two more days, you shall be free to go where you will.’

‘That’s my noble master!’ said Ariel gratefully. ‘What shall I do? Say what? What shall I do?’

Prospero told him to take the shape of a sea fairy. Only Prospero must be able to see him, but others could hear his voice.

‘Bring Ferdinand here,’ Prospero told him, and Ariel went in search of the King’s son.

Ferdinand had been washed ashore alone, on one side of the island, and he was filled with sorrow and despair because he thought that his father and all the others on the ship must have been drowned. Suddenly he heard a mysterious voice singing to him, and the words made him more miserable still, for the voice was telling him that his father was drowned, lying at the bottom of the sea. (This was Ariel's idea of a joke, and rather unkind!) Poor Ferdinand walked in the direction of the voice, and it led him on and on through the woods. What was this strange music? Surely this must be a magic island!

'Where can this music be?' Ferdinand wondered. 'Is it in the air or the earth?'

Miranda saw Ferdinand walking towards them, and she was astonished. She had never seen such a beautiful person and she felt sure he must be a fairy.

'No, he isn't a fairy,' Prospero told her. 'He eats and sleeps, just as we do. He was on the ship, and now he is looking for his father and his friends.'

Ferdinand looked up and saw Miranda, and he was certain, too, that she was no human being.

'This must be the fairy who was singing so sweetly,' he thought, and he asked her if this was so.

'No, I am human, just as you are,' Miranda answered, and Ferdinand was greatly astonished to hear her speak the same language as he did. Her gentleness and beauty made him love her at once, and she, on her side, loved him too.

This was just what Prospero had hoped for—that Ferdinand and Miranda should love each other and wish to marry.

'Delicate Ariel! I'll set you free for this,' Prospero promised, delighted. But first he wished to test Ferdinand, to make sure he was really sincere in his love for Miranda. So he spoke angrily to the young man, pretending to think Ferdinand was an enemy. He accused him of being a rival; of wanting to take Prospero's island and rule over it himself. Ferdinand denied it, and Miranda begged her father not to speak so roughly to the poor young man; but Prospero took no notice of her.

'Come with me!' he said to Ferdinand. 'I'll make you my prisoner and my slave. I'll chain your neck and feet together. I'll feed you on dead roots and sea water. Follow me!'

Ferdinand was very angry. He, a king's son, to be treated like this! It was an insult! He tried to draw his sword to fight Prospero, but he found he could not move. Prospero's magic power was too great for him, and Ferdinand decided that he could best show his love for Miranda by doing what Prospero ordered him to do. Miranda felt ashamed of her father's treatment of this gentle young man.

'Be comforted!' she said to Ferdinand. 'My father is kinder than he seems. I am sure he will not harm you.'

And so Ferdinand obeyed Prospero's command

and went to the cave. Here he was made to cut wood and carry logs, just as Caliban had to do. But he did the work cheerfully and without complaint; content because he was near Miranda.

As for Miranda, she could not understand her father's behaviour. If Prospero knew Ferdinand to be the son of the King of Naples, how dare he treat the young man like a slave? It made tears come to her eyes to think of it. Poor Ferdinand looked tired out with the unaccustomed work, and she begged him to let her help him.

'My father is hard at study,' she said. 'Pray now, rest yourself: he's safe for these three hours.'

But Ferdinand continued to work, and while he worked he told Miranda how much he loved her.

'My heart flies to your service,' he told her, 'and it is for your sake that I am this patient log-man.'

'Do you love me?' Miranda asked.

Ferdinand repeated that he did, and made her promise to marry him as soon as he could return to Naples.

'I have never before seen any man, except my father,' Miranda said, 'but I would not wish for any companion in the world except you.'

Unseen by Ferdinand and Miranda, Prospero had been listening to their conversation. He felt sure, now, that Ferdinand was a good man and would always be true to Miranda. So he appeared to them again and smiled at Ferdinand.

‘ If I have seemed cruel, it was only in order to test your love for each other,’ he said. ‘ Now I feel I can trust my daughter to your care, Ferdinand. As soon as you return to Naples you may marry her.’

Ferdinand and Miranda were overjoyed, and Prospero left them together, saying he had work to do.

Meanwhile, things had not been going so well on the other side of the island, where the rest of the ship’s party had been washed ashore. King Alonso was tired and unhappy, because he was sure his son Ferdinand had been drowned. Gonzalo, the kind old man who had helped Prospero twelve years before, tried to comfort his King by saying that Ferdinand was an excellent swimmer. The sailors had seen the young man swimming strongly towards the shore, and Gonzalo was sure that Ferdinand must have reached land somewhere. But Alonso would not be comforted. It seemed to him that they must have seen the whole island already, as they had searched for hours; yet they had not found his son.

‘ No, no, he’s gone. He is drowned,’ the King said sadly. ‘ We can search no more. Let us sit down and rest.’

Prospero’s brother, Antonio, and the King’s brother, Sebastian, were with them, and they all sat down together on the grass. They had been constantly followed by Ariel, who made loud and frightening noises around them, and their hearts were filled with fear and confusion. They were thirsty and hungry, too, but they had nothing to eat or drink, so Alonso and Gonzalo wrapped their coats around them and were soon fast asleep.

The wicked Antonio, however, was up to his old tricks. This time he was planning to kill his former friend, Alonso, and make Sebastian King of Naples in his place. Here was their chance! Alonso and Gonzalo were both sleeping peacefully and there was nobody to witness the crime. But Prospero, through his magic powers, knew what Antonio and Sebastian were planning to do. He sent Ariel to protect the king, and to frighten them all so much that they would be sincerely sorry for their past cruelty to Prospero and Miranda. Ariel arrived just in time; he found Antonio and Sebastian, their swords in their hands, standing over the sleeping king, and he wakened Gonzalo and Alonso before any harm could be done.

But the king still had to be taught a lesson, and be punished for past crimes. The puzzled men suddenly heard strange and lovely music, and Ariel and the other fairies, dressed in mysterious shapes, set a wonderful feast before them. But just as the hungry men were sitting down to eat, Ariel changed himself into a great ugly bird. He flew noisily over the table, making everything disappear as mysteriously as it had appeared. Ariel, still in the shape of the bird, spoke to Alonso, Antonio and Sebastian.

'You are three wicked men,' he said. 'And you have been brought to this lonely island because you are too wicked to live with other men.'

He went on to tell them that this was their punishment for their crime against Duke Prospero, and that only one thing could save them from death on the island. They must show sincere regret for their wickedness, and promise to lead a better life in future.

Then with lightning flaming round him and a roll of thunder, Ariel disappeared.

Alonso, Antonio and Sebastian were filled with fear and sorrow. Many violent and terrible things had happened to them within the last twenty-four hours, and they knew that the punishment was a just one. They swore they would be better men in future.

Then at last Prospero appeared before them in his magic coat. He thought they had been punished enough by all they had suffered since the beginning of the storm. At first they did not recognise him, but when he removed his magic coat and they saw who he was, they all begged his forgiveness and asked him to come back as Duke of Milan.

Prospero turned to Alonso.

'Since you have given me back my dukedom,' he said, 'I will repay you with as good a thing,' and he took him to the entrance of the cave which had been his home for so long. How thankful Alonso was when he looked inside, and saw Ferdinand sitting there with a beautiful girl! When he was told that the girl was Miranda, Prospero's daughter, Alonso begged her forgiveness for his former treatment of her father; and when he heard that Ferdinand was to marry this lovely girl, his happiness was great indeed.

'Give me your hands,' said Alonso to the two young people. 'And may all those who do not wish you well suffer pain and sorrow for the rest of their lives.'

And now the faithful Ariel led the lost sailors to their King, and they brought the news that the ship was not wrecked, as everyone had feared. The next day they all sailed back to Milan, where Ferdinand and Miranda were married and Prospero ruled again as Duke, to the great rejoicing of all his people.

Ariel flew with the ship as far as Italy, to protect it from storms, and then he was free for ever. He flew away across the sea, singing happily:

> 'Where the bee sucks, there suck I:
> In a cowslip's bell I lie;
> There I couch when owls do cry.
> On the bat's back I do fly
> After summer merrily.
> Merrily, merrily shall I live now
> Under the blossom that hangs on the bough.'

## NOTES

*Bee.* A stinging insect which sucks the sweetness out of the flowers.

*Cowslip.* A yellow flower.

*Couch.* A couch is a kind of bed. 'There I couch' means 'There I lie down to sleep.'

*Owl*, *Bat*. Both fly at night. Another name for bat is 'Flittermouse,' which means a flying mouse.

*Blossom.* Flowers.

*Bough.* A branch of a tree.

## QUESTIONS

1. Why did Prospero prefer his brother to look after the affairs of the State? How did his brother repay his trust?
2. Whom did Prospero find on the island when he arrived there?
3. Who were on the ship which was wrecked by Prospero's storm? Why did he arrange the storm?
4. Which of the ship-wrecked people arrived first at Prospero's cave, and what did he think of Miranda?
5. What happened to Ariel at the end of the story?

# JULIUS CÆSAR

## PEOPLE IN THE STORY

JULIUS CÆSAR
OCTAVIUS CÆSAR }
MARK ANTONY } faithful to Cæsar.
BRUTUS }
CASSIUS }
CASCA } among those who planned Cæsar's death.
DECIUS }
CALPURNIA, Cæsar's wife.

Two thousand years ago there lived in Rome a great soldier and leader, Julius Cæsar. He was famous all over Europe as a conqueror, and when he returned to Rome he was admired by his people as a national hero.

There were, however, certain Romans, many of them Cæsar's friends and companions, who were afraid of his increasing greatness. They suspected that he was too ambitious; that he wished to become King of the Roman people in order to gain absolute power in affairs of State.

Living in Rome at that time there was a man named Brutus. Brutus had high and noble morals and a very genuine desire to do what was best for Rome. Cæsar was his dearest friend, but Brutus watched his growing ambition with great anxiety.

Cæsar showed signs of increasing self-importance; he seemed almost to imagine that he was a god among men, and Brutus was greatly troubled.

One day Brutus met his brother-in-law, Cassius, in the street. Julius Cæsar had just gone to watch the National Games, and there would be thousands of people there. Cassius suspected that Cæsar might be offered the crown that very day. They heard the Roman people shouting in the distance, and Brutus feared the same thing.

'What means this shouting?' he said anxiously. 'I fear the people choose Cæsar for their king.'

'Do you fear it?' Cassius said. 'Then I think you would not have it so?'

'I would not, Cassius,' Brutus answered heavily. 'Yet I love him well.'

Now, Cassius was a member of the Roman Party which did not wish Cæsar to be made king, and he had been sent by his companions to persuade Brutus to join them and become their leader. As well as being a great friend of Cæsar's, Brutus was a brave soldier and a famous man, greatly loved by the Roman people, who would be more likely to follow his leadership than that of a less important man.

So Cassius started to poison Brutus's mind against Cæsar. 'Why should he think himself so great?' Cassius cried. 'I was born as free as Cæsar; so were you. We both have fed as well, and we can both endure the winter's cold as well as he. But this man is now become a god, and Cassius is a wretched creature who must bend his body if Cæsar carelessly looks at him.'

There was another great shout from the distance and Cassius, watching Brutus's troubled face, went on: 'Brutus and Cæsar: what is there in that "Cæsar"? Why should that name be more important than yours? In the name of all the gods, upon what meat does Cæsar feed, that he is grown so great?'

He paused, waiting for Brutus's reply.

'I have often thought about these things,' Brutus answered slowly, 'and I will consider what you have said. But now Cæsar is returning, so say no more.'

The two men stood in silence as Julius Cæsar passed them, and they noticed how pale and angry he looked. After he had gone, they asked Casca, another member of Cassius's Party, what was the cause of Cæsar's anger. Casca, who had been watching the Games, explained what had happened. Mark Antony, another famous soldier who had taken part in the Games, had offered the crown three times to Cæsar. Three times Cæsar had refused it, but each time he was slower in his refusal.

'Why were the people shouting?' Brutus asked, and Casca explained that they were cheering Cæsar because he had refused the crown, and this had displeased the great man. Casca was certain, that if

Cæsar were offered the crown again, he would accept it.

Brutus went home, greatly disturbed in mind. He spent a sleepless night in worrying and wondering what to do. How could they cure Cæsar of his proud nature? By what means could they save Rome from his ambitious greed? 'It must be by his death,' he at last decided sadly. 'We could never be certain how Cæsar might act if he gained absolute power.'

It was still the middle of the night when Cassius, Casca, Decius and the other members of their Party came secretly to see Brutus. Together they discussed their plans: Cæsar was to be killed the next day at the Town Hall (the Capitol) where he was going to make a speech to the people. The question was whether he alone should be killed, or whether any of his sympathisers, like Mark Antony, were to be killed with him.

Cassius said: 'I think it is not right that Mark Antony, so well beloved by Cæsar, should outlive him. We shall find him a clever and dangerous enemy.'

But the noble Brutus would not permit this. 'Antony is but a limb of Cæsar's,' he said. 'He can do no more than Cæsar's arm when Cæsar's head is off.' He shook his head and spoke with great urgency. 'I wish we could cure Cæsar's ambition without killing him, but I doubt if that is possible, so Cæsar must die. But, friends, let us kill him bravely, not angrily. We must have no bitterness in our hearts.'

So it was decided that only Cæsar should die, and, after making their last arrangements, the men went home to wait until morning.

The next day was dark and cloudy. There had been thunder and lightning all night long with terrible storms of wind, and the whole earth had shaken and trembled. Julius Cæsar, getting up after a restless night, was begged by his wife, Calpurnia, not to go to the Capitol that morning. She said she had had a most frightening dream, in which Cæsar's statue, which stood in the market place, had poured forth blood, and the Roman people came, smiling, to wash their hands in it.

'Cæsar, I used not to be superstitious,' Calpurnia cried, 'but the most fearful and unusual things happened in Rome last night. Someone saw a lion in the market place, and graves opened and gave up their dead. There was the noise of battle in the air, and the cries of men and horses in pain. O Cæsar! These things are beyond all understanding and I do fear them. I am sure they are warnings: something terrible is going to happen to you.'

Cæsar tried to comfort his wife by asking her why anything should happen to him in particular. If these strange events were really warnings, they were probably meant as warnings to the world in general and not only to him.

But Calpurnia refused to be comforted. 'When beggars die, there are no new stars seen,' she insisted, 'but the heavens themselves flash forth the death of kings.'

At last she was successful in persuading Cæsar to stay at home, but Cassius had suspected that this might happen and he sent Decius to call for Cæsar and bring him to the Capitol. When Decius heard about Calpurnia's dream, he laughed at her fears. 'Why,' he said, 'you have interpreted the dream all wrong. The blood from Cæsar's statue, in which so many smiling Romans dipped their hands, means that great Rome will suck fresh blood from Cæsar.' He turned persuasively to Cæsar. 'It means that your people will find new greatness under your rule.'

'You have explained it well,' said Cæsar.

Decius went on to say: 'I have heard that the people have decided to give this day a crown to Cæsar. If you send them word that you cannot come, their minds may change. Besides, they may make fun of you and say: "Must we wait until Cæsar's wife has better dreams?" If Cæsar hides himself, will they not whisper: "See! Cæsar is afraid!"'

How well Decius knew proud Cæsar's weakness! The leader of the Roman people could not bear to be thought a coward. He turned to his wife and said: 'How foolish do your fears seem now, Calpurnia. I am ashamed that I gave way to them.'

And wrapping his cloak about him, he went out with Decius to the Capitol.

Cæsar did not know it, but his enemies were all around him at the Capitol. One after another they made some excuse to come up to speak to him, until they all stood beside him: Cassius and Brutus, Decius, Casca, and the rest. Then, at a given signal, Casca drew his sword, crying: 'Speak, hands, for me!' and drove his weapon deep into Cæsar's back. The others quickly followed his example, and last of all came Brutus.

When Cæsar saw that even his dearest friend was against him, he cried out in despair: 'You, too, Brutus? Then fall, Cæsar!' And he fell dying on the ground.

The attack on Cæsar had taken the Roman people completely by surprise, and there was fear and confusion among them all. They heard Cinna call out, 'Liberty! Freedom! Cæsar is dead!' and watched him and the others dip their hands in Cæsar's blood; then they went half mad with fear, shouting and crying and falling over each other in their haste to get away from this terrible scene. It was now that Cassius's wisdom in choosing Brutus for a leader was proved. Brutus, the hero of the Roman people, calmed their anxious hearts. He called out: 'Do not be afraid or run away; stand still. Ambition's debt is paid. We intend no harm to any Roman.'

And the frightened people stopped and listened

to him, and when he told them that he would explain everything to them in the market place, they went quietly there and waited for him.

Meanwhile, Mark Antony, who had remained faithful to Cæsar, came to the Capitol. He spoke bitterly to Brutus, asking him if he intended to murder anyone else. 'If I myself, there is no hour so fit as Cæsar's death hour. Kill me now!'

'O Antony, beg not your death of us,' said Brutus gently. He explained that they had killed Cæsar for the good of Rome, because of his proud and ambitious nature. 'For your part, to you our swords have leaden points, Mark Antony. Our hearts receive you with brotherly love. Only be patient until we have calmed the people, who are filled with fear, and then we will explain to you why I, who loved Cæsar even when I struck him, have done this thing.'

'I loved Cæsar, too,' Mark Antony replied slowly, 'but I will wait and hear what you have to say, and hope that we may still be friends when you have given me reasons why and in what way Cæsar was dangerous.'

He asked, however, for permission to carry Cæsar's body to the market place and to make a funeral speech to the Roman people. Brutus agreed to this, and he and his friends left Antony with the body.

Antony then knelt down beside the dead Cæsar and spoke to him in bitter sorrow. 'O! pardon

'O! pardon me, thou bleeding piece of earth....

me, thou bleeding piece of earth, for being meek[1] and gentle with these butchers,' he cried. 'Thou art the ruins of the noblest man that ever lived in the tide of times.' He went on to swear that he would revenge Cæsar's murder and would have no pity for his enemies. Then, calling a servant to help him, he slowly carried the body to the market place.

Meanwhile, Brutus was already speaking to the frightened people. 'We will be satisfied: let us hear Brutus speak!' they cried, and Brutus, calling 'Be patient till the last,' began to talk to them.

'Romans and countrymen,' he began, 'you now may hear my explanation; and be silent that

[1]*meek: mild.*

you may hear. If there be any dear friend of Cæsar's here, to him I say that Brutus's love for Cæsar was no less than his. If then that friend demand why Brutus rose against Cæsar, this is my answer: not that I loved Cæsar less, but that I loved Rome more. Would you rather have Cæsar living, and die as slaves, or Cæsar dead and live as free men? As Cæsar loved me, I weep[1] for him: as he was fortunate, I rejoice at it; as he was brave, I honour him; but as he was ambitious, I killed him. There is tears for his love; joy for his fortune; honour for his bravery; and death for his ambition. I will finish with these words: I killed my best friend for the good of Rome, but I have the same sword for myself when it shall please my country to need my death.'

Brutus spoke with such honest sincerity that the people were moved to admiration. They may not have understood his high ideals, but they admired him as a man, and they cheered him from their hearts. 'Live, Brutus! Live! We'll take him to his house with shouts and praise!'

And then suddenly they were silent again, as they watched Mark Antony come slowly into the market place, carrying Cæsar's bleeding body. Brutus told them to stay with Antony and listen to his funeral speech, and the people, touched by Antony's great sorrow for his dead friend, stood and listened quietly.

---

[1]*weep: shed tears*

Mark Antony began slowly: ' Friends, Romans, countrymen, lend me your ears; I come to bury Cæsar, not to praise him. The evil that men do lives after them, the good is often buried with their bones. So let it be with Cæsar.' He paused and looked sorrowfully at the Roman people, and then went on: 'The noble Brutus has told you Cæsar was ambitious; if this is so, then it was a terrible fault and terribly has Cæsar answered for it.

' I have come, with Brutus's permission, to speak at Cæsar's funeral. Cæsar was my friend, faithful and true to me: but Brutus says he was ambitious, and Brutus is an honourable man. Cæsar was always kind and generous to the poor; he always felt great love and pity for them. Surely ambition should be made of harsher stuff? But Brutus says he was ambitious, and Brutus is an honourable man. Yesterday at the Games you all saw me offer him a kingly crown, which he three times refused. Was this ambition? Yet Brutus says he was ambitious, and Brutus is an honourable man.'

And now the Romans, moved by his words, began to turn against Brutus. 'There is truth in what Antony says,' they said to each other. 'Cæsar has been greatly wronged. Remember, he would not take the crown; therefore it is certain he was not ambitious.'

Antony went on to say that he could stir their hearts to hatred and anger, but he pretended that he did not wish to do so, ' because I should wrong the honourable men whose swords have killed Cæsar.' The people, now wholly on his side, shouted 'Honourable men! They were wicked murderers.'

And Antony spoke again: 'If you have tears, prepare to shed them now.' He showed them Cæsar's cloak[1], torn by the swords of men whom he had thought were his friends. 'See what a rent the envious Casca made!' cried Antony. 'And here the well-beloved Brutus struck. This was the unkindest cut of all. You know how dearly Cæsar loved him, and when he found that Brutus was unfaithful, his great heart broke.'

The people cried: 'O noble Cæsar! O most bloody sight! We will be revenged.'

Shouting for revenge they rushed out of the market place in search of Cæsar's murderers, and Mark Antony was well satisfied. The first part of his plan had worked.

As he was preparing to return home, a servant came to him with good news. Brutus and his friends had hastily left the city, fearing the anger of the people; and Octavius Cæsar, a General who was faithful to Cæsar, had arrived in Rome with an army at his command. Antony went at once to meet him, to make plans for battle.

Brutus and Cassius left Italy for Greece. About a year later, they were camped with their army at Sardis, and Antony and Octavius, with their army, were near the town of Philippi, some miles away.

[1]*cloak: a sort of loose coat.*

During that year, Brutus had become an unhappy, bitter man. It seemed to him that only he, out of all his Party, had killed Cæsar for a truly patriotic reason. All the others, even his brother-in-law, Cassius, were now arguing among themselves for honours, accepting bribes, and trying to gain important posts in the new Government. At Sardis that night Brutus received news that his loved wife was dead, and sorrow was added to his bitterness. He and Cassius had a quarrel: Cassius was already jealous of Brutus's leadership, as Brutus was a younger man.

In the end, however, they forgot their quarrel and began to discuss plans for the battle. They did not agree even over this. Brutus wanted to march to Philippi and attack Mark Antony there, but Cassius was against it. 'It is better that the enemy should come to us,' he argued. 'In this way he will waste his strength and tire his soldiers, while we stay here, rested and in a good defensive position.'

But Brutus pointed out to him that the people living in the country between Philippi and Sardis were sympathetic towards Antony, and many of them would join his army as it marched through their villages. He argued that their own power was at its height, and that they must strike before the enemy became any stronger.

'There is a tide in the affairs of men, which, taken at its flood, leads on to fortune,' Brutus said.

At last Cassius unwillingly agreed with Brutus, and they marched to Philippi, to the delight of Octavius and Mark Antony, who now had the advantage of a good defence position. The field of battle at Philippi was very confused, partly because both armies wore the same uniform and it was difficult to distinguish friend from enemy; and partly because there was jealousy and ill-will in Brutus's camp instead of agreement and understanding.

Cassius admitted to one of their army leaders that he had agreed to come to Philippi against his better judgment: he had great fears that they might lose this battle fought on the Plains of Philippi. Their army was tired out with the long march from Sardis; but Antony's men were fresh and rested and had already chosen the best defence positions on the Plain. Later, Cassius said the same thing to Brutus, adding: 'If we lose this battle, will you be content to be led, a prisoner, through the streets of Rome?'

Brutus swore that he would rather take his own life than allow such a thing to happen, and the two men parted, each to lead his own half of the army into battle, with their minds filled with dark thoughts of death and defeat.

The fighting went on all day, but by midday it already seemed certain that Mark Antony's was the winning side. A messenger brought news to Cassius that the enemy was in his camp, and he, mistaking Brutus's own men for Antony's, thought the battle was lost. In despair he killed himself with his own sword.

Brutus, arriving on the scene a short time later, found his brother-in-law dead, and he cried out bitterly: 'O Julius Cæsar, thou art mighty[1] yet! Thy spirit walks abroad, and turns our swords against ourselves.'

He felt hopeless, thinking that all was lost, but he bravely led the remainder of his army once more against the enemy. Before long he was defeated and, although he and a few friends managed to escape, most of his army was taken prisoner.

Mark Antony told his soldiers to treat the prisoners with every kindness. 'I had rather have such men my friends than enemies,' he said. He then gave orders that Brutus must be found and brought to Octavius's tent.

But when Brutus at last was found he also was dead, killed by his own hand and with his own sword, like Cassius. All his hopes for the glory of Rome, all his honest efforts for the good of the Roman people, seemed to him to have failed miserably, and he felt he had nothing more to live for.

Mark Antony, kneeling beside Brutus's body, felt a great unhappiness for the wasted life of this fine and honourable man.

'This was the noblest Roman of them all,' he said. 'All the others did what they did in envy

---

[1]*mighty: powerful.*

‘ This was the noblest Roman of them all ’

of great Cæsar; Brutus was the only one with honest thoughts for the good of the people.’

He stood up and told his soldiers to carry Brutus’s body into the camp for honourable burial. ‘ We must treat him according to his virtue,’ he finished, ‘ and say to all the world: “ This was a man, a brave and honourable man.” ’

QUESTIONS

1. Why did a certain Party of Romans wish to kill Julius Cæsar?
2. Why did Calpurnia beg Cæsar not to go to the Capitol?
3. What two reasons did Antony give to show that Cæsar was not ambitious?
4. Why did Brutus decide to march from Sardis to Philippi?
5. Why was Brutus ‘ the noblest Roman of them all ’?

# KING LEAR

## PEOPLE IN THE STORY

KING LEAR
GONERIL, REGAN, CORDELIA — his daughters.
DUKE OF ALBANY, Goneril's husband.
DUKE OF CORNWALL, Regan's husband.
KING OF FRANCE, DUKE OF BURGUNDY — who wish to marry Cordelia.
EARL OF KENT
EARL OF GLOUCESTER
EDGAR, EDMUND — Gloucester's sons.

ONCE, many hundred years ago, there was a king of England called Lear. He had ruled his land well and wisely for many years, but now he was growing old and feeble and he felt that it was time for the kingdom to pass into younger hands. So he decided to give up his title, and spend the rest of his life in quietness and peace.

Lear had no son to succeed him, but he had three daughters, Goneril, Regan and Cordelia, and his plan was to divide the kingdom among them. Goneril and Regan were already married, Goneril to the Duke of Albany, and Regan to the Duke of Cornwall; and there were two visitors to Lear's court—the King of France and the Duke of Burgundy—both of whom were anxious to marry Lear's youngest daughter, Cordelia. The old king thought that his daughters, with good husbands to help and advise them, would be able to rule England as well and wisely as he had done.

Lear had already decided which share of his kingdom was to go to each daughter, but before telling them of his decision he sent for them and asked each in turn whether she truly loved him. Goneril, the eldest, answered him first. 'Sir,' she said, 'I love you more than words can say. You are dearer to me than eyesight, life or liberty. No child has ever loved her father more than I love you.'

The king, perhaps a little weak and foolish in his old age, was well pleased with this speech, not realizing its insincerity. He called for a map of England, and pointing to it said: 'Of all these bounds, from this line to this, I make you ruler. Yours and Albany's children will be your heirs.' Then he turned to Regan and said: 'What does our second daughter, our dearest Regan, say? Speak.'

And Regan answered in the same insincere way as Goneril. 'My feelings are the same as my sister's,' she told her father, 'but she has not expressed half the love I feel for you. I am only happy when I am able to serve you.'

The old king smiled fondly at her and gave her, also, a third of his kingdom. At last he turned to Cordelia, his dearly loved youngest daughter.

‘Of all these bounds, from this line to this I make you ruler....

‘What can you say to deserve your share?’ he asked her gently.

Now, Cordelia had listened to her sisters’ speeches with increasing anger, knowing that they were only praising the old king so excessively because of their greed for their share of the kingdom. She, who truly loved her father, could not bear to have her real love compared with their false pretence. And so she answered a little bitterly: ‘I love you as I should: neither more nor less.’

Lear looked at her in astonishment, and cried: ‘You had better mend your speech, Cordelia, or you may lose your fortune.’

But Cordelia answered quietly: 'My lord, you are my father. You have cared for me, fed me, and loved me: for these reasons I obey you, love you and greatly honour you. Why have my sisters married, if they say they love no one but you? If ever I have a husband, half my love and duty will belong to him.'

'Do you mean this with all your heart?' asked her amazed father, and Cordelia answered that she did. 'So young and so untender!' Lear said sadly. He found it hard to believe that his youngest daughter, who had always seemed to love him so greatly, had really only felt a sense of duty towards him.

The tired old king, hurt and unhappy at this unexpected speech by his favourite child, grew angry.

'If this is the truth,' he cried, 'then truth can be your dowry[1]. You will get nothing more from me.' Turning to his smiling elder daughters, he divided Cordelia's share of the kingdom between them. 'As for you,' he said bitterly to Cordelia, 'I disown you for ever. You are no longer a daughter of mine.'

King Lear had a good and faithful courtier, the Earl of Kent, who now tried to persuade him to change his mind. But Lear interrupted him with angry words and, after a bitter quarrel, told Kent

---

[1]*dowry: marriage gift.*

to leave his kingdom for ever. So Kent left the court, calling upon the gods to shelter poor friendless Cordelia.

Lear then called the two visiting noblemen, the King of France and the Duke of Burgundy, who wished to marry Cordelia.

'There she stands,' he said, pointing to Cordelia. 'Her only dowry is my curse. She is no longer heir to any part of my kingdom. Do you still wish to marry her?'

Burgundy tried to persuade the king to give Cordelia her share of the kingdom, but when this was refused he said he could not marry her.

'Peace be with Burgundy!' said Cordelia. 'And since it is my fortune that he loves, and not myself, I shall not be his wife.'

The King of France, however, gave a different answer.

'Fairest Cordelia,' he said gently, 'you are most rich, being poor. I love you for your virtues and your beauty.' He turned to Lear and said: 'Your penniless daughter, King, thrown to my chance, is queen of us and ours, and our fair France.'

'Take her,' replied Lear. 'Let her be yours, for she is no daughter of mine, and I shall never see her face again. Be gone, without my love or blessing.'

Cordelia said goodbye to her sisters, and begged them to take good care of their old father; but they jealously told her to look after her own husband, and not try to teach them their duty. So Cordelia left the court with the King of France; but she was troubled about her father, fearing that his elder daughters might not treat him kindly.

Her fears were soon proved to be just. According to his plan, the old king was to live first with one daughter and then with the other. He would keep the title of King, and would have a hundred of his own knights to attend him. He first visited his eldest daughter, Goneril, and her husband, the Duke of Albany. He was his daughter's guest only, and had no authority over her servants. He soon found that all Goneril's protestations of love towards him were false. She made no effort to attend to her father's needs and make him comfortable in her palace. She complained that he was always finding fault with her servants and ordering them about, and that his knights behaved as if they owned the place. She allowed her own servants to treat the king and his knights with careless rudeness, and they took no notice of his orders, pretending not to hear them. At first the old man could not believe that Goneril was neglecting him intentionally, but he was soon forced to realise that he was not being treated with the respect due to a king. It seemed to the unhappy old man that everyone was against him; even his court jester[1], the amusing fellow who was paid to keep the king cheerful and in good heart, was amusing no longer, now that

[1]*jester: joker.*

Cordelia had gone away. The poor Fool had loved her and missed her sadly.

But there was still someone who was anxious to help the old king in his loneliness. The Earl of Kent, when sent from the court, had not gone far away and now he returned, dressed as an ordinary servant. He had changed his appearance, so that no one recognised him, and he told Lear that he would like to work for him and would serve him faithfully.

'All right,' said the king. 'If I like you no worse after dinner, you may stay with me.'

So Kent stayed with the king, and he very soon had an opportunity of proving his usefulness. One of Goneril's servants spoke very rudely to the old man, and the king lost his temper and struck him. This was, of course, an unfortunate occurrence, as it made Goneril angry; but the faithful Earl of Kent (or Caius, as he now called himself) supported the king's action and knocked the servant down calling him 'you base football player.'

Goneril's behaviour to her father grew daily worse; she was determined to drive him away from her palace by her unkindness, because she did not want the trouble and expense of keeping him and his hundred knights. Lear at last realised that she did not want him, and said bitterly: 'Are you my daughter?' He called for his knights, and then turned to Goneril again. 'I'll trouble you no longer,' he said to her. 'I still have another daughter who, I am sure, is kind and comforting. I will go to Regan.'

The Duke of Albany, a good and kindly man who was unfortunately too weak-willed to go against his wife's wishes, now begged Lear to be patient. 'My lord,' he said, 'I am guiltless. I do not know what has angered you.'

'That may be so,' Lear answered hotly, 'but I'll stay here no longer, to be treated so unkindly by my own daughter.' He turned and cursed Goneril with bitter, heart-broken words, finishing: 'How sharper than a serpent's[1] tooth it is to have a thankless child! Away, away!'

When his knights gathered round him, he found that his cruel, strong-willed daughter had already dismissed half of them. He now had only fifty followers, instead of a hundred. And so the old king left the palace, accompanied by his fifty knights and the faithful Earl of Kent (or Caius), and followed by the Court Fool, who ran after him crying: 'Nuncle Lear, nuncle Lear! Wait, and take a fool with thee.'

Lear could not believe that his second daughter, Regan, would behave as badly as Goneril had done, and he set off for her palace, sending Caius on ahead with a letter to tell Regan of his arrival. But when he reached her palace, Caius found that Goneril had also sent a letter to her sister, and Regan and

---

[1]*serpent: snake.*

the Duke of Cornwall had decided to leave their home rather than to stay there and receive the king. They had gone to the castle of the Earl of Gloucester, and Caius followed them there and gave them the king's letter.

While he was waiting for their answer, Caius met the same servant whom he had called 'a base football player' and knocked over for his rudeness to Lear at Goneril's house. They had another quarrel and a fight, and Caius was taken prisoner. By the orders of the Duke of Cornwall, and against the will of the Earl of Gloucester (who loved his old king and did not wish to harm Lear's servant), Caius was put 'in the stocks': an old form of punishment, where a man was made to sit outside, no matter how bad the weather was, with his hands and legs imprisoned through the holes of a wooden framework.

Caius was left in the stocks all night, and here he was found by King Lear the next morning. The king, very angry at this cruel treatment of his servant, went at once to Gloucester's castle to speak to Regan and her husband. He could only find the Earl of Gloucester, however, who told him apologetically that Regan and her husband refused to see Lear, saying that they were tired and ill after their journey. Here was the first sign that Regan was going to treat her father as rudely as Goneril had done, but Lear could not believe it. When Regan and the Duke of Cornwall came at last to welcome him, he at once told them about Goneril's unkindness, feeling sure of Regan's sympathy.

But this daughter was as cruel and unloving as the other. 'I pray you, sir, have patience,' Regan said. 'I cannot think that my sister would fail in her duty towards you. I am sure she had good reasons for all she did, and is not to blame in any way.'

Lear interrupted her angrily, but she continued: 'O, sir, you are old; you should be ruled and led by others who are younger and wiser than yourself. Go back to Goneril, and admit that you were wrong.'

'Am I to ask *her* forgiveness?' Lear cried. 'Must I say to her: "Dear daughter, I am old, and old age is unnecessary; I beg you on my knees for clothing, bed and food"?'

But Regan had no sympathy for him; nor could he get any answer to his question as to who had put Caius into the stocks. And then Goneril herself arrived, and Regan again told the old king to go back to her. 'I am now away from home,' she said to him. 'I cannot entertain you when I myself am only Gloucester's guest.'

But the king refused to return to Goneril. He said that he and his fifty men would stay with Regan. Regan replied, however, that she could only take in twenty-five of his knights; in fact, said she, what need had he of any? Her own servants could look after him.

And Lear at last realised, to the full, the wickedness and greed of his two elder daughters. He called upon the heavens to give him strength and patience. 'You see me here, you gods, a poor old man, wretched with age and sorrow,' he said. 'Teach me to bear my daughters' cruelty with a noble anger. Let no tears stain my face!' He turned wildly to his two stony-hearted daughters. 'You think I'll weep,' he cried. 'But no, I'll not weep! I have every reason for weeping, but my heart shall break into a thousand pieces before I'll weep. O Fool, poor Fool!' He turned to his faithful jester. 'Come, let us go. I think I am going mad.'

And he slowly left the castle, supported by the Fool and Caius, and walked out into the stormy night.

In their wanderings, Caius lost sight of the old king, who now had only the Fool to help him. They wandered through the storm together in search of shelter. In the open, treeless countryside they had no protection from the wind and the rain, and the old king's mind was as cold and wandering as his body; he was slowly going mad with sorrow.

Caius, after a long and anxious search, found them at last and took them to a broken-down old hut where they could shelter for the night. The old king was, by this time, so disturbed in mind that he did not notice the storm, and Caius had difficulty in persuading him to enter the hut. When at last they went inside, they found that the hut was already occupied by a poor mad fellow who called himself 'Poor Tom,' and kept crying out 'Tom's a-cold' and singing foolish songs. Old Lear, wandering in his mind, thought this poor mad man must have been treated like himself. 'Did you give everything to your two daughters?' he asked him. 'And are you too come to this?'

Now, 'Poor Tom' was really the elder son of the Earl of Gloucester: a good and faithful young man who had been turned out of his father's house because of the wicked lies of his younger brother, Edmund. Edmund was jealous and ambitious, and had turned their father against Edgar because he himself wished to become heir to the Earldom of Gloucester. And now Edgar, driven away from his home, had changed his appearance and pretended to be a mad man, in order to avoid recognition and imprisonment.

The Earl of Gloucester, ashamed of Regan's treatment of Lear, was wandering the countryside in search of the old king, and during his absence the wicked Edmund was planning against his father and his king.

Lear had not been long in the hut when the Earl of Gloucester found him, and, with the help of Caius and Edgar (whom he did not recognise), the Earl took the king to a farmhouse near his castle. Later, Caius—who had now shown himself as the Earl of Kent—took Lear secretly to his own castle at Dover, a town on the south coast of England opposite the coast of France. The Earl of Kent then sailed across to France and told Cordelia about her father's sufferings, and the wickedness of Goneril and Regan. Cordelia persuaded her husband, the King of France, to send an army to England to fight for King Lear, and she herself crossed to Dover with the army.

The good Earl of Gloucester had his eyes put out by Regan and the Duke of Cornwall, as a punishment for helping Lear. They then turned him out of his castle; but the faithful Edgar, still pretending to be 'Poor Tom,' led his father to Dover, where they joined King Lear. The poor old king was sadly changed: he had now gone quite mad, and did not recognise them. He talked strangely, and wandered about wearing a crown of leaves and flowers.

Nor did he recognise Cordelia when he first saw her again; but gradually his madness disappeared. 'I am a very foolish fond old man,' he said to Cordelia, 'and I fear I am not in my perfect mind. I think I should know you, yet I am doubtful.' He looked unhappily at the people round him, still fearing that he might receive unkindness. 'Do not laugh at me,' he begged them. 'Perhaps I am being foolish, but I think this lady is my child Cordelia.'

'Oh, I am, I am!' cried Cordelia, overjoyed that her father knew her at last.

He talked strangely, and wandered about wearing a crown of leaves and flowers

But the sorrowful old man, remembering her sisters' unkindness to him, could not believe that Cordelia still loved him. 'You have some reason for not loving me. They had none,' he said.

But Cordelia told him that her one wish was to bring him back to happiness, and he said gently: 'Forgive and forget: I am old and foolish.'

The time had come for the two enemy armies to meet: the French army, led by Edgar and the Earl of Kent; and the English one, led by the Dukes of Albany and Cornwall and the wicked Edmund. Goneril and Regan went with their husbands, chiefly because they wanted to be near Edmund.

This evil young man wished to become King of England, and so he made love to both Goneril and Regan, in the hopes that he would, in the end, be able to marry one of them, and so gain possession of half the kingdom.

In the battle which followed, the French army was unfortunately defeated, and Lear and Cordelia were taken prisoner by the wicked Edmund. He sent them to prison and gave secret orders that Cordelia was to be killed. He was determined that she—one of the rightful heirs to England—should not stand between him and his ambition to be king.

Meanwhile, there was hatred and bitterness in the English camp. Regan's husband had died, and she immediately announced that she intended to marry Edmund; but Goneril, angry and jealous, poisoned her sister and Regan also died. And now the Duke of Albany, whose greatest fault had been his weakness of will, turned against his wicked wife. He sent her to prison for her crimes, and she killed herself in anger and despair. Finally the evil Edmund was killed in battle by his brother Edgar.

The Earl of Kent was able to tell all this to King Lear, but it is doubtful whether the old man understood the news. His mind had failed again when Cordelia died, and he could not be persuaded to leave her body.

'She's gone for ever!' he cried despairingly. 'She'll come no more—never, never, never, never!'

And the broken-hearted old man fell dead beside his beloved daughter.

And so ended, in sorrow and despair, the long life of the good King Lear; but, although he seemed to have lost everything, the battle had not been in vain. His two wicked and cruel daughters were dead, and also the ambitious Edmund. The crown passed to the Duke of Albany, who became king of all England. Helped by Edgar, who became Earl of Gloucester when his old, blind father died, and by the good Earl of Kent, the Duke of Albany ruled well and wisely, and England became a rich and peaceful land once more.

## QUESTIONS

1. Why did King Lear decide to divide his kingdom among his three daughters?
2. What answers did Goneril and Regan give to his questions as to whether they truly loved him?
3. Why did Cordelia give him a different answer?
4. Who were Caius and 'Poor Tom'?
5. How did Goneril and Regan treat their old father?
6. Why did Goneril poison Regan?
7. Who gave orders for Cordelia to be killed? What happened to him in the end?

# MACBETH

## PEOPLE IN THE STORY

DUNCAN, King of Scotland.
MALCOLM / DONALBAIN } his sons.
MACBETH / BANQUO } Generals of the King's army.
MACDUFF, a Scottish nobleman.
LADY MACBETH.
THREE WITCHES.

ONCE, many years ago, there was a Scottish nobleman named Macbeth. He was the Thane (or Lord) of Glamis, and a cousin of Duncan, King of Scotland. Macbeth was a general in the king's army, a brave man and a fine soldier; and at the time the story opens he was fighting for the king against the King of Norway and a wicked Scottish Lord, the Thane of Cawdor. In the battle, the Thane of Cawdor was taken prisoner and the Norwegian king was forced to surrender; and the victorious Macbeth returned to the king's palace with his friend and fellow-soldier, Banquo.

On their way back from the battle-field, they had to cross an open treeless stretch of country called a heath. The day was dark and stormy, but suddenly a flash of lightning showed three mysterious figures standing in front of the two men.

' Who are these, so strange and wild in their appearance?' said Banquo in surprise. ' They do not look like human beings.'

The three strange old women stood in silence, their fingers to their lips, and Macbeth said sharply: ' Speak if you can. What are you?'

Now, as Banquo had suspected, these women were not human beings but witches: strange creatures who had the power to see into the future, and to speak of matters which had not yet occurred. The first witch now addressed Macbeth as ' Thane of Glamis,' but the second called him ' Thane of Cawdor,' and the third made an even more sur-

She said to Macbeth: ' You will be King of Scotland '

prising statement. She said to Macbeth: 'You will be King of Scotland.'

While Macbeth and Banquo stood speechless with surprise, the witches turned to Banquo and said: 'Your sons will be kings, although you will not.' And then, with a flash of lightning and a roll of thunder, the three old women disappeared.

Banquo turned to Macbeth in amazement. 'Did we really see three mysterious old women?' he asked. 'Or have we eaten some poisonous root which has turned us mad?'

'They said your children will be kings,' Macbeth said slowly, and Banquo added: 'And you will be king.'

'And Thane of Cawdor, too,' said Macbeth. 'Didn't they say that?' He shook his head doubtfully. 'The Thane of Cawdor is still alive. And how could I ever become king? Duncan has two sons. The old witches must be wrong.'

But as they stood there, wondering at the strange words they had heard, two noblemen came riding across the heath towards them. They brought the surprising news that King Duncan, wishing to reward Macbeth for his bravery in battle, had made him Thane of Cawdor, in place of the wicked Thane who had been taken prisoner and sentenced to death.

And thus the first words of the old witches had already come true. Macbeth said softly to Banquo:

'Do you hope your children will be kings? It was promised to you by those old women who said I should be Thane of Cawdor.'

Banquo was greatly troubled. He called the mysterious witches 'the instruments of darkness,' and said that he feared their words. He felt that Macbeth might try, by wicked means, to make himself king; he might have a superstitious feeling that it was a natural course, because the witches had sworn that it would happen. And Banquo's fears were right. The witches' promise had planted a seed of wicked ambition in Macbeth's mind, and the influence of their words is seen in all the events that follow.

Meanwhile, King Duncan wished to show Macbeth great honour, and decided to visit him at his castle. Macbeth asked permission to go home at once, to prepare for the royal visit; but before he left the palace he sent a letter to Lady Macbeth, his wife, telling her about the strange witches and how the first part of their promise had already come true.

Now, Lady Macbeth was a very ambitious woman, more cruel and determined than her husband. She at once made up her mind that Macbeth should become king, and that the quickest way to achieve this was to murder King Duncan. Duncan was already on his way to visit them, and it seemed to her that Fate was on her side. Those 'instruments of darkness,' so greatly feared by the honest and noble Banquo, were already influencing this ambitious woman.

When Macbeth arrived, she at once told him her plan. She said Macbeth must welcome the king with great friendliness. 'Bear welcome in your eye, your hand, your tongue,' he said. 'Look like the innocent flower, but be the serpent under it. Tonight we will arrange his death.'

Macbeth was filled with doubts, his anxious mind a mixture of hope and fear. How could he murder Duncan, who was not only his king but his cousin and his guest? But his hard-hearted wife said firmly: 'All you have to do is to give him a royal and friendly welcome. Leave the rest to me.'

The king arrived that evening, and after a meal he went early to bed. Macbeth, making one last fight against ambition, said to his wife: 'We will go no further in this business. The king has done me great honour and I cannot deceive him.'

But Lady Macbeth had made her plans, and she would let nothing stand in her way. 'Are you a coward?' she said angrily. 'Will you give up your chance of becoming king, just because you are afraid?'

'But if we fail....' Macbeth argued uncertainly.

'Screw up your courage to the highest point, and we'll not fail,' said Lady Macbeth, and told Macbeth her plan. She would give Duncan's two guards so much strong wine to drink that they would become drunk and stupid. Then, when they were all sleeping, she and Macbeth would murder the king, and put the blame on the drunken bodyguard.

Late that night, when everyone in the castle was asleep, Lady Macbeth crept quietly to Duncan's room with a dagger[1] in her hand. She feared her husband's weakness and was determined to murder the king herself. But when she saw him lying there asleep, something in his face reminded her of her father, and she found she could not kill him. She returned to Macbeth, gave him the dagger, and told him to do the deed.

After a few moments he returned to her, shaking with fright. 'I have done the deed,' he cried. 'But didn't you hear a noise?'

Lady Macbeth tried to calm him, but he went on: 'Someone laughed in his sleep, and another cried "Murder!" I thought I heard a voice cry "Sleep no more! Macbeth does murder sleep."'

'What do you mean?' said Lady Macbeth sharply, and Macbeth went on, his voice full of fear: 'I tell you, someone cried "Sleep no more! Glamis has murdered sleep, and therefore Cawdor shall sleep no more; Macbeth shall sleep no more."'

'You must have been dreaming,' said Lady Macbeth angrily. 'Go and wash the blood from your hands.' And then she noticed that he had brought the blood-stained daggers with him. 'Why

[1] *dagger: short pointed sword.*

did you bring these?' she asked. 'You must go back and leave them beside the sleeping servants, as a witness that they have done this crime.'

'I'll go no more!' cried Macbeth wildly. 'I am afraid to think what I have done. I dare not look on it again.'

'Infirm of purpose!' said his wife. 'Give me the daggers.' And she went back to Duncan's room to put the daggers on the floor beside the sleeping servants.

In a few moments she returned, and showing Macbeth her blood-stained hands she said: 'My hands are of your colour, but I should feel ashamed to wear a heart so white.'

When the murder was discovered the next morning, the castle was filled with horror and confusion. Macbeth, as soon as he was told the news, went straight to Duncan's room and killed the two servants, pretending that he did it because they had killed their king and master.

The news of Duncan's death was quickly carried to his two sons, Malcolm and Donalbain, and they, feeling sure that the servants were innocent and Macbeth guilty of the crime, hurriedly left Scotland. Macbeth took advantage of their flight and claimed that they must be guilty of the murder and must have paid Duncan's servants to do the deed. Macbeth was now Duncan's nearest relative in Scotland, and therefore heir to the kingdom, and he was crowned king at once.

And thus the witches' second promise had come true; but Macbeth was not yet satisfied. The witches had also said that Banquo would be father to a line of kings, and Macbeth felt that Banquo and his son were a constant danger to him. So he and Lady Macbeth arranged to have a feast for the chief Scottish nobles, and they invited Banquo and his son to stay at the castle as their guests. Macbeth then hired two wicked men to murder them while they were out riding on the afternoon of the feast. The murderers, however, only succeeded in killing Banquo; his son escaped to England, and many years later there was a line of Scottish kings descended from him. Thus the third promise of the witches did, in the end, come true.

The feast began in spite of the fact that Banquo and his son had not appeared. One of the murderers had returned and told Macbeth that Banquo was dead, and Macbeth was not greatly troubled by the news of the son's escape. He considered that Banquo had been his most dangerous enemy. He knew that his former friend had strong suspicions about him, having witnessed the scene with the witches. Now that Banquo was dead Macbeth felt more secure, and he went in to the feast with a cheerful heart.

When he reached the table, however, there did not seem to be a place for him. Someone was sitting in his chair. He looked more closely, and saw to his horror that it was the ghostly spirit of

To his horror he saw that it was the ghostly spirit of Banquo

Banquo. No one else could see the ghost, and when Macbeth cried out in fear his guests thought he must be ill. Lady Macbeth encouraged this belief, explaining, 'My lord is often thus, and has been since his youth.' She then took Macbeth aside and scolded him, with hard and bitter words, for being such a coward. The ghost disappeared, and Macbeth controlled himself and sat down at the table.

'Give me some wine. Fill my glass!' he said to a servant. 'I drink to the general joy of the whole table, and to our dear friend Banquo whom we miss.' He held up his glass but once again his face turned pale with horror. The ghost of Banquo had appeared again. This time Macbeth could not control himself, and he spoke so strangely that Lady Macbeth thought it would be wiser to ask the guests to leave. Macbeth looked so wild and strange that she was afraid he might give away their terrible secret.

After the guests had gone, Macbeth decided he would once more visit the three witches to see if they could offer him any more advice. He had gone so far in crime to satisfy his own wicked ambition; he had already murdered four people—Duncan and his two servants and Banquo—and he felt that he could not turn back now. What was done could not be undone, and he was prepared to kill others in order to protect his own safety. Macbeth was sure that there was one nobleman, at least, who suspected his crimes. This was Macduff, the Thane of Fife. Macduff, too, should be killed if necessary.

Early next morning Macbeth set out for the lonely heath where he and Banquo had first met the witches. This time the old women gave him warnings as well as promises. The first warning proved that his fears concerning Macduff were right.

'You must watch Macduff, the Thane of Fife,' they said; but their next words brought comfort to Macbeth's anxious heart, because they went on: 'You need not fear the power of man. No man born of woman can harm Macbeth.'

And lastly they said: 'Macbeth shall never be

conquered until great Birnam Wood to high Dunsinane Hill shall come against him.'

Dunsinane was a castle surrounded by a dense forest called Birnam Wood, and the witches' words put Macbeth's superstitious mind at rest. How could trees uproot themselves and attack him? The old women must mean that he would never be conquered!

However, Macbeth decided to play for safety; the witches had warned him against Macduff, and so Macduff must die. Imagine his anger, therefore, when he was told on his return to his castle that Macduff had gone to England to join Duncan's son, Malcolm. In his anger, Macbeth sent two evil men at once to Macduff's castle, ordering them to murder Lady Macduff and her children.

Meanwhile, in England, Macduff and Malcolm were making plans to fight Macbeth, and when Macduff received the news of the murder of his family he determined to be revenged on their murderer without delay. He and Malcolm marched at once to Scotland with a strong army to attack Macbeth. Many Scottish nobles had grown to hate Macbeth for his cruelty and wickedness, and they joined Malcolm's army as soon as it crossed the border from England.

Macbeth moved to Dunsinane Castle, which had strong defences, and gathered an army together. There were times when he was almost in despair. Since Duncan's murder he had not known one moment of peace and happiness, and Lady Macbeth's mind was failing under the strain. She had urged her husband to start on his path of crime; she had driven him unmercifully, her strong will keeping a continuous watch on his weaker one. Now the strain was proving too great. Her nights were filled with terrible dreams, and she wandered round the castle in her sleep, talking strangely and trying to wash imaginary stains of blood from her hands. 'Yet here's a spot!' she would cry in despair. 'Who would have thought the old man had so much blood in him?' And then she would talk of Lady Macduff and Banquo, her poor unhappy mind filled with a sense of guilt. The doctor could find no cure for her, and before long she killed herself in sorrow and despair.

Macbeth began to realise how empty his life was. He had hoped to gain so much when he was king, but he had gained nothing and lost everything: his friends, his honour, the trust of his soldiers, and his wife's companionship. 'I have lived long enough,' he thought sorrowfully. 'Those things which should accompany old age, such as honour, love, obedience, a faithful army, good friends—all these things I cannot hope to have. Instead, I must expect hatred and curses from everyone.'

But the news came that Malcolm's army was near at hand, and Macbeth was stirred to courage. 'I'll fight them all!' he cried. 'I will not be afraid of death till Birnam forest comes to Dunsinane.'

He prepared to meet the enemy, but before he had time to leave the castle a messenger came running to him with the most astonishing news. 'As I was watching upon the hill,' he said, 'I looked towards Birnam, and suddenly I thought the wood began to move.'

'You are a liar!' cried Macbeth, in terrible anger. 'Such a thing cannot be true.'

But it was true. Malcolm had told his soldiers to cut down some of the trees in Birnam Wood and carry the leafy branches in front of them. In this way their advance would not be noticed, and the number of their soldiers would be hidden from the enemy.

The witches had said: 'Fear not till Birnam Wood comes to Dunsinane,' and now the wood seemed to be moving towards the castle. Macbeth began to understand how the three evil witches had deceived him with their false promises; but there still remained one more promise: 'No man born of woman can harm Macbeth.' Surely there could be no deceit in that?

And so Macbeth, who had never lacked courage as a soldier, went out to meet the enemy. He fought with great courage, and his belief in the witches' promise gave him confidence.

Macduff, leading the enemy army, was determined to fight and kill Macbeth, to revenge the murder of his wife and children. So when he saw him, he rushed towards him shouting: 'Turn,

Macbeth, turn!' Macbeth, remembering Lady Macduff and her helpless children, cried: 'Get back, Macduff. I have already killed too many of your family.' Macduff, however, continued to attack him, and they fought fiercely.

At last Macbeth said: 'You are wasting your strength, Macduff. I have a magic life which no one of ordinary human birth can take from me.'

'You can despair of that magic,' answered Macduff. 'I was not born in the ordinary way. I was taken from my mother by an operation before the time was due for my birth.'

Then Macbeth knew that the witches had deceived him to the end. He cursed them bitterly, and lost both hope and courage for a moment. 'I will not fight with you,' he cried to Macduff.

'Then surrender, coward!' said Macduff scornfully, 'and we will make a show of you to everyone, and tell them what a cruel, evil man you are.'

At these words, Macbeth recovered his courage and cried: 'I will not surrender to kiss the ground before young Malcolm's feet, and be cursed by the common people. Lay on, Macduff, and cursed be he who first cries "Hold, enough!"'

In the fight that followed Macbeth was killed, and his strange unhappy life came to an end. Malcolm was crowned King of Scotland, and Macduff was made the Earl of Fife as a reward for his faithful service to his king.

## QUESTIONS

1. At their first meeting on the heath, what two promises did the witches make to Macbeth?
2. Why was Banquo doubtful and troubled about the promises? Was he right in his fears?
3. Whom did Lady Macbeth plan to blame for Duncan's death? What did she give them to make sure they would not wake up that night?
4. What did Macbeth see at the feast which frightened him so much?
5. At their second meeting on the heath, the witches promised Macbeth two things. Say what they were, and explain why Macbeth was deceived by false hopes.

## MACMILLAN STORIES TO REMEMBER SERIES
## SENIOR TITLES

A Tale of Two Cities *by Charles Dickens*
Alice in Wonderland *by Lewis Carroll*
Anna of the Five Towns *by Arnold Bennett*
Coral Island *by R.M. Ballantyne*
David Copperfield *by Charles Dickens*
Dr Jekyll and Mr Hyde *by R.L. Stevenson*
Emma *by Jane Austen*
Far from the Madding Crowd *by Thomas Hardy*
Great Expectations *by Charles Dickens*
Hard Times *by Charles Dickens*
Jane Eyre *by Charlotte Bronte*
Journey to the Centre of the Earth *by Jules Verne*
Kidnapped *by R.L. Stevenson*
Lord Jim *by Joseph Conrad*
Persuasion *by Jane Austen*
Pride and Prejudice *by Jane Austen*
The Adventures of Huckleberry Finn *by Mark Twain*
The Black Arrow *by R.L. Stevenson*
The Count of Monte Cristo *by Alexandre Dumas*
The Greatest Tales of Sherlock Holmes *by Arthur Conan Doyle*
The Greengage Summer *by Rumer Godden*
The Mill on the Floss *by George Eliot*
The Moonstone *by Wilkie Collins*
The Red Badge of Courage *by Stephen Crane*
The Return of the Native *by Thomas Hardy*
The Scarlet Pimpernel *by Baroness Orczy*
The Three Musketeers *by Alexandre Dumas*
Three Shakespeare Tragedies
Tom Jones *by Henry Fielding*
Twenty Thousand Leagues Under the Sea *by Jules Verne*
Vanity Fair *by W.M. Thackeray*
Wuthering Heights *by Emily Bronte*